Morning Briefings

Daily Wisdom and Inspiration
from Scripture

Change your world by bringing God into it every day!

Written by Christine DiGiacomo

xulon
PRESS

Morning Briefings
Daily Wisdom and Inspiration from Scripture
by Christine DiGiacomo

Printed in the United States of America

ISBN 9781628391701

Unless otherwise indicated, Bible quotations are taken from the following:

Amplified Bible (AMP)
Copyright © 1954, 1958, 1962, 1964, 1965, 1987 by The Lockman Foundation

English Standard Version (ESV)
The Holy Bible, English Standard Version Copyright © 2001 by Crossway Bibles, a division of Good News Publishers.

Holman Christian Standard Bible (HCSB)
Copyright © 1999, 2000, 2002, 2003, 2009 by Holman Bible Publishers, Nashville Tennessee. All rights reserved.

The Message (MSG)
Copyright © 1993, 1994, 1995, 1996, 2000, 2001, 2002 by Eugene H. Peterson

New King James Version (NKJV)
The Holy Bible, New King James Version Copyright © 1982 by Thomas Nelson, Inc.

www.xulonpress.com

Six years ago, Christine was contacted by a local businessman, seeking answers to some spiritual questions, as they related to business—particularly running his international company in such a way that he might glorify God. After several meetings, it became clear that he and his business partner would profit from digging deeper into God's Word on a daily basis. How? With demanding schedules that included business, international travel and families. . .how would they make that happen? That was when Christine began writing daily e-mail Bible studies, sending five days a week, teaching straight through Scripture, functioning as the company's corporate pastor. From those first two businessmen, the "Morning Briefing" readership has expanded to 127 countries and thousands of readers. . .something only God could have made happen!

Here is the first collection of Morning Briefings from Paul's inspirational writings to the Philippians and Colossians, meant to be read daily – to grow in knowledge of God, his Word and basic discipleship. They are printed in the same format—e-mail-style—in the way they have been distributed these last six years. Christine draws on her 18 years of Bible teaching, conference and retreat speaking, experience as director of women's ministries, leader of Fellowship of Christian Athletes at her local public high school, more than a decade of Women of Passion, (an ecumenical community Bible study), and from her vantage point of being a wife and mother of four children. Her writing is passionate, clever, oft-times personal and certainly timely for the challenging and exciting climate of today's living.

From: Christine DiGiacomo,

To: you, the interested reader,

**Subject:
a daily dose of wisdom
from Scripture.**

From: Christine DiGiacomo <espressocd@cox.net>

Subject: Peace that brings the smile of contentment. Philippians 1.1-2

Peace is a sought-after thing—often elusive in this day and age. Now I am not talking about the absence of war, or the absence of violence, but rather the state of inner tranquility, of serenity. Actually, peace is peddled in many ways, and people are willing to do just about anything to get it! Aromatherapy, self-help books, yoga, relaxation, stress-relief techniques, self-hypnosis, essential oils, light therapy . . .we chase after these methods to try to achieve a sense of calm. And don't forget the big business of anti-depressants, sleeping pills, and anxiety meds! Plus, have you noticed that the power of positive thinking is being touted again?

The only peace that is worthy of the name is **Peace with God**. God's peace is not man-made, can't be trumped up with enough good will, can't be bought or read about in a book. Our loving God offers his children a peace that surpasses all understanding! His peace makes it possible for me to be in a trying, very difficult situation, and defying all logic, still know peace. God's peace cannot be adequately described. However, if I asked you to define God's peace, and you have experienced it, your first thought would etch a sweet smile on your face—your entire countenance would change just thinking about God's peace.

Paul writes about peace that surpasses all understanding in the book aptly named "Philippians". And so we open our Bibles to the latter part of the New Testament, turning the pages carefully, so as not to miss the four short chapters. There . . .did you find it? It is right in there with the other letters Paul wrote from prison. Wait—prison? Yes, Paul wrote this letter to the church at Philippi while he was in prison in Rome.

Why did Paul write to the Philippians? He had established a church there about 10 years earlier, and while in this Roman prison, those sweet people from Philippi heard, and sent someone to take care of him, tend to his needs, and in essence, love Paul for them. Of all of the churches Paul had established, he enjoyed the sweetest relationship with this Philippian church; oh, how he loved them! And they loved him; they were devoted to him because they understood that Paul had brought them life—not through oppressive Rome, or through the Jewish Law, but through the saving grace of Jesus Christ.

Paul dictates, "Paul and Timothy, servants of Christ Jesus, To all the saints in Philippi, together with the overseers and deacons; Grace and peace to you from God our Father and the Lord Jesus Christ." Philippians 1.1-2

Notice with me that Paul begins his letter by saying who was writing to them—just the opposite of our letter-writing style—we sign our names at the end. He claims Timothy as having the same thoughts and heart as he does, since Timothy had been with him on his original visit to Philippi. Paul refers to the Christians at Philippi as 'saints'—those who were leading lives, changed because of their relationship with Jesus Christ. He also references overseers and deacons, so quite obviously since Paul had originally founded the church, it had experienced a lot of growth.

"Grace and Peace through God our Father and the Lord Jesus Christ," he extends. We know that both grace and peace flow from the heart of our Heavenly Father, made possible through Jesus' sacrifice on the Cross. But there is more to this chosen expression of 'Grace and Peace.' Paul combines two normal greeting phrases of his day—those of the Greeks and the Hebrews. Charis is the greeting the Greeks used to begin all of their letters, while Shalom is the greeting the Jews used to greet one another. Used together, we see how both are enriched by the other because of the influence of the Good News of Jesus Christ. When Paul prays for grace and peace on the people he loves, he is praying that they will have the joy of knowing God as Father, and the peace of being made right with God, to others and to themselves. . .and friends, here we see it—Grace and Peace can only come through Jesus Christ. Amen.

'Want peace in your life? 'Want the smile of inner contentment on your face? Follow Jesus, and follow him closely. And this study of the book of Philippians is sure to aid you in a deeper understanding of the peace and joy in growing closer and closer to your Lord.

Grace and Peace to you!
Christine

From: Christine DiGiacomo <espressocd@cox.net>

Subject: The Heart of God meets Philippi. Philippians 1.3

The heart of God meets Philippi. Philippians 1.3

The heart of God is so full of love we have no way of comprehending it.

The heart of God desires one thing—to love and be loved by humanity.

The heart of God shows no partiality; he is an equal opportunity lover.

There is no partiality with God, Paul wrote. Or as another translation of the same verse states it, God pays no attention to this world's distinctions.[1]

The church at Philippi serves as a grand expression of God's heart. (captured in Acts chapter 16) The story of Paul's stay in Philippi centers around three people—three very different people. But before we discuss them, let's consider Philippi herself. Paul was quite strategic about the places he chose to preach, so why Philippi? The city was a commercial center in the ancient world for several reasons: location, gold and silver mines, Philippi's status as a Roman colony, and maybe most importantly, the main road that traveled through the town, which linked Rome with her eastern provinces. All of which made it a prime location for the introduction of the good news of Jesus Christ.

Upon arriving in a new town, it was Paul's custom to go first to the synagogue, but there was none in Philippi, which indicates there were few Jews in town. And so the missionaries went to the river just outside of town to look for a place of prayer.[2] At the river, Paul does indeed find a small group of the faithful. Lydia, a successful businesswoman whose business was 'purple' was among this prayerful group. Purple?? She traded in purple garments—purple, in fact, came from her home town of Thyatira.[3,4]

The men sat down and told the group about the Savior; Lydia opened her heart to Jesus Christ, along with her household, and was baptized. (That was quite handy to be next to a river!)

So grateful to Paul, Lydia insisted, 'Come and stay at my house'. And she persuaded us, Paul noted.

First convert in Philippi – Lydia.

Day after day, as the new Christians and Paul made their way to the river for fellowship and prayer, a demon-possessed slave girl would shout their presence as they walked through town. (Can you picture that?) "Finally Paul became so troubled that he turned around and said to the spirit, "In the name of Jesus Christ I command you to come out of her!"[5] And it left . . .along with the money she made for her owners fortune-telling. Utt-oh.

Her owners grabbed Paul and Silas and brought them before the authorities, who ordered them to be beaten with rods and thrown into prison. The jailer was sternly warned to carefully guard them, so he put both battered men in stocks down in the inner prison. But about midnight as Paul and Silas were praying and singing praise songs to God, there was a great earthquake which caused the jail doors to be opened, and chains to fall off. (Look at God's response to Paul and Silas's prayerful praise!) Sure that Paul and Silas had escaped, the jailer prepared to kill himself, until Paul shouted, 'No . . .we are all here! Do not harm yourself.'

The jailer yelled for someone to bring him a torch so he could see, and looked at Paul and then Silas, and realized that he wanted to know the God they served. After all, these men were like no others he had ever encountered! After being forcefully beaten, stretched out on stocks in the cold damp prison cell, they praised their God! That was anything but normal—peace, joy even while they suffered? And well, he reasoned with himself, 'it had to be God who caused that earthquake!' 'Please tell me how I can be saved!' he urgently pleaded. To which Paul responded, "Believe in the Lord Jesus, and you shall be saved, and your household." The jailer and all of his family members put their trust in Christ that night, and were baptized, adding to the number of Christians in that town called Philippi.

"I thank my God every time I remember you," Paul wrote in his letter to the friends he had made there—three of whom we are now aware—the wealthy Asian businesswoman, Lydia, the set-free Greek slavegirl, and the Roman jailer. Paul's heart mirrors the heart of God, who loves and draws each and every one of us to himself . . .no partiality, no consideration of gender, race, or social status. God just does not play favorites, and I for one, am glad!

Grace and peace,
Christine

1) **Romans 2.11**
2) **When there was no synagogue in town, or it was unsafe for Jews to openly worship God, it was customary to go outside the city and establish a 'place of prayer', often by a river.**
3) **Purple dye was derived from the shellfish in the waters of Thyatira;**
4) **Thyatira is present day Akhisar, Turkey;**
5) **Acts 16.18**

From: Christine DiGiacomo <espressocd@cox.net>

Subject: Community–the place of doing life together. Philippians 1.3-8

Good Morning!

Who notices when you aren't there? I mean, maybe besides your family . . .does anyone really care how you are doing? Who encourages you to keep the faith when the going gets tough? When you are sick, does anyone call to check on you? If you moved out of the area, would you leave a void, or would no one likely notice? Has anyone 'been there' for you when life tossed you about, such that you did not know up from down? Hmmm . . .

On the other hand . . .may I ask, who do **you** encourage? Have you recently reached out to lend a hand, or send a note, to someone who is hurting? When is the last time you brought a meal to someone in need? Do **you spend** much time praying for the heartfelt needs of others? Have **you** had the opportunity to extend the handshake of 'welcome' to another lately? Have you walked alongside' some friends that have weathered the rough storms of life, and seen them through to the other side? I mean, how often do you GIVE of yourself to others? Hmmm . . .

The answers to the above questions are two sides of the same coin—they are the reflections of your involvement in the lives of other people, and vice versa. If you could answer in a mostly positive manner, it is likely that you are part of a community of Christian faith. Yes, a community of Christian faith. If you found yourself wondering who, if anyone, would 'be there' for you . . .and struggled to remember the last time you 'were there' for someone else, you seriously need to

>consider finding a community of believers that you might join<

Paul writes, 'I thank my God every time I remember you. In all my prayers for all of you, I always pray with joy because of your partnership in the gospel . . .it is right for me to feel this way about all of you, since I have you in my heart. . .' I can <u>completely</u> identify with Paul's feelings for the Philippian believers to whom he was writing! A little more than a decade ago, when my family moved from Northern to Southern California, I left behind a close-knit community of Christian women that I had built, then built up, then led for three years. In our new home a week, boxes unpacked, everything was fine . . .until my household got busy with their new assignments: Matthew was a senior and Amy a junior in high school, Dylan was a kindergartner, and Danny, 2 years old, hung with his mama. Dean resumed his job. . .What about me? Then I realized, I had moved far away from my community—the women I had loved, encouraged, and nurtured in the Lord; women who had loved and encouraged me. . .and I missed them dreadfully! They were my community, and I was cut off from them, and I don't think I had never been so lonely before.

How about now? Well, similarly, I have led Women of Passion for about 13 years now . . .we have studied, prayed, laughed, cried, ministered, celebrated, mourned, and retreated together. If I had to move away from them . . .well, I would experience an even greater loss—as our time together, and mutual investment in one another and the kingdom of God, has been longer and deeper. Like Paul, I would give thanks for them, and I would always carry them in my heart . . .

And then there is the band of brothers, of which I am one—my corporate guys. For six years we have studied, prayed, fasted, praised and sought God together. I care deeply for them—in a way that the world could never comprehend or understand. It is right, it is pure, it is godly, and it is God-honoring. It is an authentic community where the seven of us find safety, sharpening, acceptance, accountability, encouragement and trust—we are a cord of three strands, which as the writer of Ecclesiastes says, is not easily broken. So, yes, I understand Paul's heart toward the Philippians:

"I thank my God every time I remember you. In all my prayers for all of you, I always pray with joy because of your partnership in the gospel from the first day until now, being confident of this, that he who began a good work in you will carry it on to completion until the day of Christ Jesus.

It is right for me to feel this way about all of you, since I have you in my heart and, whether I am in chains or defending and confirming the gospel, all of you share in God's grace with me. God can testify how I long for all of you with the affection of Christ Jesus." Philippians 1.3-8

Friend, do you belong to a band of brothers? Are you part of a group who will lift you before the Father in prayer? Oh, I pray so! If not, may I encourage you, in the strongest terms possible, to search one out. Find a community, join it, and make it better. Communities do life together—particularly the Christian life.

Grace and Peace to you, MY sweet community . . .
Christine

From: Christine DiGiacomo *espressocd@cox.net*

Subject: wHen lovE doeS not a-B-o-u-N-d.
Philippians 1.9

I had been looking ahead, anticipating talking about love in today's Morning Briefing . . .Paul's love for the Philippians, and because of his heart full of good will for them, how it was his earnest desire that their love would continue to grow and deepen and . . .well as he said himself, "I pray that your love may abound more and more . . ." So yesterday, I sat there on the stationary bike at the gym, looking up from the Scripture rubber-banded to the rack in front of me, staring off into space thinking, 'well, why wouldn't their love keep growing?' And then . . .'hmmm . . . well, why does love get hindered any way?'

Moving on, I had things outlined in my mind, just the way I was going to proceed. (Yes, it seems that no matter my activities, I am always carrying notes with me, and chewing on ideas in the back of my head—sometimes wrestling with notions about various things, and piecing things together . . .) So, when I left the gym this morning, I was ready to go. But rather than sitting down at my computer to start today's briefing, I decided to hem a pair of pants before heading out for two ministry meetings; I would write a bit later. All that to say, I had the local news on the radio as I did so; otherwise, I never would have had the 'luxury'(?) of hearing the coverage of a most dreadful local police/criminal case.

Here's the story: in early July, a homeless man died . . . allegedly at the hands of city policemen. An investigation ensued, and today, the district attorney held a news conference to announce the charges, and the reason for them. [It was somewhat unusual for me to catch something like this, particularly the 'live' coverage of it . . .] With careful attention to detail, the DA described the video coverage of one policeman, in particular, demanding that the schizophrenic, homeless man—known by these policemen, and most folks in the community—follow his instructions to sit first this way, and then that . . .and though the man was obviously confused, the officer donned rubber gloves, made fists, and told him he was "going to _ _ _ him up", and then did. . .complete with help from another officer who tased him, and then, beat him in the face eight times with the taser gun . . .

I felt physically sick as I listened. 'Oh, God, this is so sad . . .this was all so avoidable,' I breathed, as I pressed a crease into my pants. Let's just take the one policeman, viewed by 151 witnesses and captured on three videotapes, doing more or less what I described above . . .whatever in the world took place in this man's life that he would conduct himself like this toward another human being? What made him think that the life of this man was worth nothing? What made him think he had the right to wield life or death that day, while charged with the task of 'protecting the public'? 'Oh God, forgive us . . .how we have erred in our esteem of life!'

Segue back to our passage when Paul said, 'I pray that your love may abound . . .' What happened to love in this batterer's life? Was love limited to his wife, his mama, his children? Or does he not really know how to love them, either?

Oh, I suppose this case especially breaks my heart because of the time I spent in Long Beach, coming alongside homeless, often mentally ill people . . .because of listening to some of their stories, because of so many of them being so terribly misunderstood. And somehow in the midst of their 'being misunderstood', to others they were devalued as human beings; they ceased to be "fearfully and wonderfully made" as our loving Creator said they were! See, I get it . . .when you do not know folks personally, you can see them en masse as 'the crazy homeless', or 'those lazy beggars', or 'derelict addicts' . . .when the truth is, NO ONE WOULD CHOOSE THAT LIFE. No one would choose to go to sleep with his head on the concrete, sweatshirt rolled up beneath him.

So, what happened to Mr. Second Degree Murder/Mr. Involuntary Manslaughter Policeman with regard to LOVE? I do not know. But I will tell you what did not happen. He did not grow up knowing a loving God, because if he did, his heart would not be void of love and compassion for God's children. He does not now walk with a loving Lord, because he could not ever mistreat His creation with no conscience . . .those two are mutually exclusive! Why, you cannot walk with God, and hate the lives of others, to the point that you would hurt, harm, nay . . .even kill them!

So, like Paul, "I pray that YOUR LOVE may abound more and more . . ." your love in God the Father, and the Lord Jesus Christ . . .your love, one for another, that you may grow in grace and love. And I pray that as you grow in the love of God that you will give it away . . .that it will spread and be an all-consuming fire in a world that can be cold, hate-filled, and most un-lovely.

Go and LOVE,
Christine

From: Christine DiGiacomo <espressocd@cox.net>

Subject: A treasured letter. Philippians 1.9-11

Twenty-one hundred miles from home . . .and upon my arrival, not knowing a single soul. It was quite an experience—mostly a good one. See, I had chosen to go to a Christian liberal arts college in St. Paul, Minnesota, far away from my Northern California home. Getting adjusted to the Midwestern 'take' on things was probably my biggest adjustment, besides missing my mom, my piano, and my big black dog. One thing was a source of continued joy while I was there—a letter from Home. I read it, reread it, and then stuck it in one of my college textbooks and carried it with me. I treasured the written connection from my mom and dad, as I pictured them sitting down at the kitchen table to write a letter to their little girl, far away from home.

Ah yes, those letters were treasures.

I knew my loving mother and dad pictured me as they wrote; just so, Paul pictured his Christian friends in the Philippian church. Indeed, as he wrote from his cell in the Roman prison to express his gratitude for their faithfulness to Jesus Christ, and their continued love and support for him over the last decade since he had been able to be with them, he pictured some of their familiar faces. Ah, how he loved them!

Meanwhile, in Philippi, and as is the custom, believers have gathered to worship God. Among the faithful that meet in Lydia's home, there is a buzz in the air because the word is out—a letter has arrived from Paul! Oh, how they adored their beloved pastor!

Lydia smiles as she welcomes her dear ones, and remembers to herself: 'Why, it seems just yesterday that I was praying with the women at the river, when Paul and Silas and the others joined us. At first, we were wary of the strangers, until we listened to Paul. I had never heard anything like it—and he got this other-worldly look on his face as he told us about how Jesus got his attention while he was traveling to Damascus. Paul told us of the joy he had known in his heart ever since that time, and I leaned in closer so as not to miss a word. He told us what it was like to experience the presence of God in his heart and life—no Jewish teacher I had ever heard talked like this man! He really had our attention, and then went on to tell us that his experience was not for him alone, but that Jesus Christ wanted to have the same relationship with us. . .that we too could become followers of this Jesus Christ. Oh, I shall never forget that day—it was the day of my rebirth—the day that I met my Lord, and was baptized into the Christian faith.

So much has happened since then. Just looking around, it is not just those women and me anymore, but many others have become a part of our gospel community. Ah, now someone is about to read Paul's words to us—'Brothers, sisters, a messenger delivered this letter from our brother Paul; I know you will treasure its words just as I have since its arrival. Do not forget, Paul drafted this letter to us from a Roman prison; I cannot even imagine the depth of his love for Jesus Christ, and for us, that he would go to such lengths to send us encouragement, when he himself is in that torture chamber!

"I thank my God every time I remember you. In all my prayers for you, I always pray with joy because of your partnership in the gospel from the first day until now . . .It is right for me to feel this way about all of you, since I have you in my heart; for whether I am in chains or defending and confirming the gospel, all of you share in God's grace with me. God can testify how I long for all of you with the affection of Christ Jesus." Uh, allow me to interject something here—for all of you who sacrificed your own comfort to send provisions to Paul, you see how much it meant to him! You see how much it aided him in his travels to spread the good news of the gospel—the same good news that he had brought to us all those years ago.

Permit me to continue reading, brothers. "And this is my prayer: that your love may abound more and more in knowledge and depth of insight, so that you may be able to discern what is best and may be pure and blameless until the day of Christ, filled with the fruit of righteousness that comes through Jesus Christ—to the glory and praise of God."

What do YOU think Paul meant, in praying that 'their love would abound more and more . . .'? We will continue to look at this treasured letter to the Philippians, but I must ask you—since you came to know Jesus, has your love come to abound more and more?

Think on this—
Christine

From: Christine DiGiacomo *espressocd@cox.net*

Subject: Paul prays the perfect prayer.
Philippians 1.9-11

Several weeks ago, I asked for prayer as I endeavored to 'launch' Fellowship of Christian Athletes at my nearby San Clemente High School. Someone stopped me at the gym the other day, and said, 'Hey, how is it going? How is it going at the high school?' Because I requested your prayer, it is only right that I tell you about what is happening; so today, I wish to give an accounting . . .

First, do you pray for your son or daughter, or some young person you care about? What informs your thinking about how to pray? Are you concerned that you are not praying the 'right things', or not covering 'all the bases'? Or, are you at the helm of a group of people, attempting to steer them—hopefully toward good and right things, and if you have the liberty, toward a life filled with joy, meaning and purpose in God? Please keep reading.

How about San Clemente High School? Well, we launched FCA three weeks ago at the locals' favorite beach in town . . . Riviera! (see http://pastorwoman.com/ReadArchive.aspx?id=744) . . . God was there. Two more Sunday nights have followed at different venues, with each evening drawing between 60 and 70 students, and a lot of interest. Check this out: I know of several dynamic, intelligent young people who have never been introduced to Christianity who are coming and even wanting to serve, just so they can hear about what it means to be a Christian. Does it get any better than that? I submit to you that it does not!

Then, last week, FCA was approved to be an on-campus club as well, with about 150 students signing up to attend—at Club Rush, our table drew the most attention and response. So tomorrow, (Tuesday), bi-monthly lunch time meetings begin. Oh, God is good. He is faithful.

At a time in our culture, when there is so much over which to be concerned, to see young people desire to know God, and come together to do so—well, it is something to jump up and down about! MTV, Youtube, Facebook, Text-Messaging even, may have a deleterious effect on the minds of our youth in many ways, but right now Facebook and Mass Text Messaging, (along with word of mouth enthusiasm), are the vehicles through which God's messages are being peddled at our huge public high school. Gotta love it.

At the helm of a group ***you*** want to lead well? Got young people for whom ***you*** wish to pray? Want to pray a powerful, yet practical prayer for those **you** love? Look with me at how Paul prays for the Philippian believers:

"And I pray this: that your love will keep on growing in knowledge and every kind of discernment, so that you can determine what really matters and can be pure and blameless in the day of Christ, filled with the fruit of righteousness that [comes] through Jesus Christ, to the glory and praise of God." Philippians 1.9-11

Paul prays for his dear friends, that they will grow in all areas of love . . .(hmmm . . .when I pray for my children, I do not think to pray that love will grow in their lives . . .) Yet 'love' is a repeat theme in Paul's writing, and here we see him apply it as though he might be talking about wisdom! Huh—who was it that said that 'love is blind'? On the contrary, LOVE sees with eyes wide open, and loves in spite of, in full view of, and sometimes, upon truly seeing, loves another back to health, or loves another in such a way that change and healing may be possible. One rendering of this verse is "My prayer for you is that you may have still more love—a love that is full of knowledge and every wise insight".

So, let us pray as Paul did—the perfect prayer for another
~ That your love will keep on growing:
~>in knowledge – understanding of what is at hand;
~>in discernment – that it may be proven what is wise; that one may use keen judgment;
~>so that you can determine what really matters – establish priorities
~>and be pure and blameless when Christ comes;
~>known for righteousness – the ability to choose what is right, and do it in Jesus Christ, to glorify God the Father.

Paul prayed the perfect prayer for the Philippian believers . . . but it is also the perfect prayer for your children, for the small group you lead, and for my dear FCA students whose hearts are being drawn to God. Oh, what a passage! Oh, what a prayer that Paul has given to us! Yes, Friends, 'holy men of God spake as they were moved by the Holy Ghost.'[3] Which is why—two thousand years later—in the worldly culture of Southern California, these words still have application; which is why, my dear ones who read from Pakistan, Singapore, the Philippines, Germany, and Ghana—these words still apply! That you may grow in love of our Christ Jesus—a love that is wise, discerning . . .and well, so much more.

May God add his blessing to the impartation of his precious Word. Amen.

Christine

From: Christine DiGiacomo <espressocd@cox.net>

Subject: Wisdom meets Love. Philippians 1.9-11

God's Word came alive again for me! (Yes, Mr. Hebrews, the 'Word of God <u>is</u> living and active'![1]) Here's what I mean: I was studying and writing about what I dubbed 'Paul's perfect prayer' in verses 9 through 11 of Philippians 1, and I could not help but notice a similarity in terms. Paul prayed for his loved ones to have more love in their lives—which would produce knowledge and discernment and the ability to choose the "excellent". Consider with me again Paul's words:

"And this I pray, that your love may abound still more and more in real knowledge and all discernment, so that you may approve the things that are excellent, in order to be sincere and blameless until the day of Christ; having been filled with the fruit of righteousness which comes through Jesus Christ, to the glory and praise of God." (NASB)

Let's think about this—with more of God's love in the believers' lives, that love would produce knowledge, discernment, and the ability to choose the 'excellent' . . .It appears that Love has just met Wisdom.

What is wisdom? The wisdom God supplies has several components:

>__understanding__–what is true, right, lasting
>__discretion__–the ability to decide responsibly
>__prudence__–wise in handling practical matters, exercising good judgment, common sense, careful about one's conduct
>__discernment__–keen insight
>__knowledge__–the body of wise teaching
>__action__ – in exercising discretion, prudence, or discernment in a course of action. It may surprise you to see 'action' linked with wisdom, but what good is any of the above qualities of wisdom, if once you see things clearly, you fail to exercise it? Wisdom must therefore impact our actions.

Hmmm . . .why yes, there is quite a connection between love that comes from God and the wisdom of God. We read in Proverbs, 'The fear of the Lord is the beginning of wisdom, and knowledge of the Holy One is understanding.'[2] And from the apostle John, 'Dear friends, let us love one another, for LOVE COMES FROM GOD. Everyone who loves has been born of God and knows God.'[3]

The connection of love and wisdom is unmistakable. The reason? Both emanate from God. Truly, **Love and Wisdom are founded in the heart of God.**

Our Lord's half brother, James, told us that if we ask God for wisdom, he will give it to us.[4] You and I can and ought to ask God daily for his wisdom—that we might be discerning, prudent, etc.

May I boldly challenge you to start your day with prayer? Set apart an area of quiet, and commune with your Father. If Jesus made doing this a priority, oh, how much more do you and I need to do it! Include praise, a time of confession, and then begin your petitions/your requests by asking God for wisdom . . .that you may have understanding, knowledge, discretion, discernment, prudence and the presence of mind to execute them?

Ask God to grow his love in your life . . .that you may choose what is excellent. Fully developed love never travels alone. It is accompanied by all the other virtues. It functions in beautiful cooperation with full knowledge and keen discernment.[5] How good, how right! Love is blind? Bah! Love is perceptive, and when it meets wisdom, gives the heart and mind the ability to separate not only good from bad, but also, the important from the unimportant.

Dear Father, I pray for my friends around the world right this moment . . .I pray, Lord God, that you would grow their love for you exponentially, in such a way that it cannot help but flow over into the lives of others. I pray that you would cause them to turn to you, the Author of Wisdom, and ask, that they may receive! And having received the wisdom from above that is pure, then peaceable, gentle, open to reason, full of mercy and good fruits, impartial and sincere,[6] they might bring honor to you from their lives. Amen.

Grace and Peace, Christine

1 Hebrews 4.12–Look these up, and write them out: _____
2 Proverbs 9.10–_____
3 1 John 4.7–_____
4 James 1.5–_____
5 William Hendriksen, <u>New Testament Commentary: Exposition of Philippians</u>
6 James 3.17–_____

From: Christine DiGiacomo <espressocd@cox.net>

Subject: That your love will keep on growing . . .this is my prayer for you.

True love finds its roots in God, our Father. 'Pretty hard to be 'filled to overflowing' with love unless you grasp in some part the magnitude of God's love for you. Do you have any idea how much he truly loves you? He looks at you as his **beloved**.

You are the Beloved. You are much loved by God. And being the Beloved expresses the core truth of our existence.

I am putting this so directly and so simply because, though the experience of being the Beloved has never been completely absent from my life, I never claimed it as my core truth. I kept running around it in large or small circles, always looking for someone or something able to convince me of my Belovedness. It was as if I kept refusing to hear the voice that speaks from the very depth of my being and says: "You are my Beloved, on you my favor rests." That of course is what God the Father said to his Son, and what I have to hear from him each day of my life.

Perhaps the voice has always been there, perhaps not. Growing up in the home of very old-school parents, in a conservative Protestant church, I do not remember being told that I was much loved by God—at least in such a way that I could 'get it'. Or perhaps I was more eager to listen to other, louder voices saying: "Prove that you are worth something; do something relevant, spectacular, or powerful, and then you will earn the love you so desire." Meanwhile, the soft, gentle voice that speaks in the silence and solitude of my heart remained unheard or, at least, unconvincing.

I think you understand what I am talking about. Aren't you, like me, hoping that some person, thing, or event will come along to give you that final feeling of inner well-being you desire? Don't you often hope: "May this book, idea, course, trip, job, country, or relationship fulfill my deepest desire." But as long as you are waiting for that mysterious moment you will go on running helter-skelter, always lustful and angry, never fully satisfied. You know that this is the compulsiveness that keeps us going and busy, but at the same time makes us wonder whether we are getting anywhere in the long run.

You and I don't have to kill ourselves. **We are the Beloved**. We are intimately loved long before our parents, teachers, spouses, children, and friends loved or wounded us. That's the truth of our lives. That's the truth I want you to claim for yourself. That's the truth spoken by the voice that says, "You are my Beloved."

Listening to that voice with great inner attentiveness, I hear at my center words that say: "I have called you by name, from the very beginning[1] You are mine and I am yours[2]. You are my Beloved, on you my favor rests. I have molded you in the depths of the earth and knitted you together in your mother's womb[3]. I have carved you in the palms of my hands[4] and hidden you in the shadow of my embrace. I look at you with infinite tenderness and care for you with a care more intimate than that of a mother for her child.[5] I have counted every hair on your head[6] and guided you at every step[7]. Wherever you go, I go with you, and wherever you rest, I keep watch[8]. I will give you food that will satisfy all your hunger and drink that will quench all your thirst.[9] I will not hide my face from you[10]. You know me as your own as I know you as my own. You belong to me.

Nothing will ever separate us.

For I am convinced that neither death nor life, neither angels nor demons, neither the present nor the future, nor any powers, neither height nor depth, nor anything else in all creation, will be able to separate you from my love that is in my Son, Christ Jesus your Lord.[11]

This has fresh application again for me—which the truths of God always do. In a number of situations, including e-mails which come from countries I would be challenged to locate on a globe, people are crying out to be convinced of the love of God for them.

And so I close with, 'You are the Beloved of God.' Give yourself over to that truth, give yourself over to the lordship of the God who always has YOU on his mind. For then you shall surely see the answer to Paul's prayer—to my prayer for you—that your love may abound more and more.

Grace and Peace,
Christine

A lot of this text came from <u>The Life of the Beloved</u> by Henri Nouwen. He really speaks to my heart.

1 from Isaiah 43
2 Song of Solomon 6.3
3 from Psalm 139
4 Isaiah 49.16
5 1 Thessalonians 2.7
6 Matthew 10.30
7 Proverbs 16.9
8 Psalm 121.4
9 Psalm 81.10, 16
10 Psalm 27
11 Romans 8.38-39, personalized

From: Christine DiGiacomo <espressocd@cox.net>

Subject: God always has a plan. Philippians 1.12-14

Christianity was in trouble . . .or so it seemed. The spreading of the Gospel had come to a screeching halt . . .or so it seemed. The teacher, the pastor, the main man had not just been arrested, but he had been transported to Rome, and was being held in tight security. Was this the end of the faith already? If so, the persecution new believers endured would only be greater, and they would seemingly be without hope.

Paul knew his Philippian brothers wondered about these things, but they also worried for him because of the great love and affection they held for Paul.

And so he sends word to those he loved, those he carried in his heart . . .

"I want you to know, brothers, that what has happened to me has resulted rather in the advancement of the gospel, because it has been demonstrated to the whole Praetorian Guard and to all the others that my imprisonment is borne for Christ's sake and in Christ's strength; and the result is that through my bonds more of the brothers have found confidence in the Lord the more exceedingly to dare fearlessly to speak the word of God."
Philippians 1.12-14

How could this be? Paul is saying his imprisonment would actually extend the Gospel, not shut it off? Indeed. His incarceration in Rome was part of God's plan. In Acts 28, we read that Paul was shackled to a member of the Praetorian guard, (from Caesar's household), at all times.[1] Every four hours, there would be a changing of that guard, while Paul was awaiting his trial before the emperor. Ultimately, Paul was permitted to arrange his own private lodging while he waited for two years for his 'court date', but he was still chained to a soldier at all times. Think of it—over the span of two years, how many of these guardsmen heard the Gospel . . .why they could probably repeat it in their sleep! All the Praetorian Guard knew why Paul was imprisoned, and they saw his courage, conviction, and undying loyalty to Jesus Christ. They could not help themselves—many of them were touched by Paul's Lord . . .also their families . . . even extending to Caesar's house.

When Christians throughout the Roman Empire heard how cleverly God used Paul's incarceration, it actually served to embolden them! It gave them fresh courage to tell others about Christ, and so the Gospel spread through this means as well.

I have been thinking—if I were arrested, would one of you carry on the work I do, endeavoring to share God's Word, locally and globally? I am not claiming to be a 'Paul', but hey, Sisters, in my Women of Passion community, if the sheriff arrested me and put me in Orange County jail, how would that affect you? Would you just say, 'Oh well, too bad for her', and go your own way? Or, would you become an activist for the cause of Christ?

To my corporate brothers, if I were no longer able to lead you in conference call prayer meetings, and face-to-face Bible studies, send you Bible studies . . .would you pick up the baton and advance God's Word?

Last night, I stood before a group of more than a hundred high school students and answered the question, 'how do I grow in my faith?' When I had asked the Lord for the best direction to take, I felt he said, 'Just give them Jesus—just give them Me!' And so I took them to John chapter 15—many of them finding a passage in the Bible for the very first time!—I showed them Jesus' words, 'I am the Vine, you are the branches. . .' and explained that all true spiritual growth comes through Christ, and being connected to him. 'How do you get connected and stay connected to Jesus?' Meet him in his Word, and learn to pray. I had their rapt attention as I told them what truly moved me to become a praying woman, filled with faith—it was seeing God's work in my life, as he actually answered some specific prayers I had lifted to him in very powerful ways! I showed them what simple daily prayer can look like, but also explained that prayer is the real work of an individual's life that will be as relevant and life-giving at 53 years of age, as it is at 15 years of age.

The bonds I am forming with these young people who crave the truths of God are other-worldly. From what I teach them, they are writing about it, and posting on Facebook, for the world (and their fellow high school peers) to see! If I were snatched away, the Word of God would keep going through them—I truly believe that.

There are pockets and whole movements of 'underground' Christians who must literally answer this question for themselves—if my teacher were to be taken away, what would my reaction be? They already risk their lives by stealing away in the dark of night to meet in 'safe' places to hear God's Word, and then their Bible teacher is arrested, tortured and put in a work camp . . .what then? Is that the end to their Christianity? No! It usually galvanizes more people to share the Word of God, and the work of Christ. And yes, guards in their torture chambers often come to know the life-saving message of Jesus Christ, watching the faith of these persecuted, mistreated believers.[2]

God always has a plan . . .for the Philippian church, for Paul, and for the spread of Christianity—in the first century and today.

Grace and Peace, Christine

1) Acts 28.16
2) Such as the story of Brother Yun in *The Heavenly Man*

From: Christine DiGiacomo <espressocd@cox.net>

Subject: You are now free to move about the country
Philippians 1.15-18

'You are now free to move about the country' . . .'One of the clever advertising lines of Southwest Airlines. But it also might have been the feeling of some of Paul's contemporaries when Paul was held captive in Rome. In the preceding few verses, Paul commented that the Gospel was still being preached, though he was unable to move from town to town himself. However, Paul is certainly no one's fool—he is well aware that some who stepped forward to preach while he could not, did so out of impure motives.

"It's true that some are preaching out of jealousy and rivalry. But others preach about Christ with pure motives. They preach because they love me, for they know I have been appointed to defend the Good News. Those others do not have pure motives as they preach about Christ. They preach with selfish ambition, not sincerely, intending to make my chains more painful to me. But that doesn't matter. Whether their motives are false or genuine, the message about Christ is being preached either way, so I rejoice. And I will continue to rejoice." Philippians 1.15-18

Oh, you' gotta love Paul. Astute enough to see the opportunists pounce on their big chance to gain influence with the people, since he was no longer able to 'move about the country'—yet, able to rejoice because, in spite of their motives, the good news of the Gospel was still being preached.

Paul never campaigned to be the emperor, but rather, called himself the servant of the Lord Jesus Christ. All that mattered to Paul was that the work of the cross—the freedom available to all through the free grace of God—was taught. This same Paul had written to the church at Corinth, "Though I am free and belong to no one, I have made myself a slave to everyone, to win as many as possible . . .To the Jews I became like a Jew, to win the Jews . . .To the weak I became weak, to win the weak. I have become all things to all people so that by all possible means I might save some."[1]

Note that those to whom Paul was referring (while he was captive in Rome) were preaching the gospel: that *Jesus had come,* (as the fulfilllment of the prophecies of old), lived, taught, loved, and died willingly on the Cross, a perfect sacrifice for our sins, once and for all; he rose from the grave, and ascended into Heaven, to sit again at the right hand of God the Father. He has commented on the ***motive*** of the opportunists who tried to gain notoriety while he was incarcerated, not their ***message***.

If the message is right, that is what matters most to Paul. If the cause of Christ is going forward, that is the important thing. That is no different for us today; whether some sit, others kneel, some sing hymns, others sing contemporary worship songs . . .what difference does it make? They are worshiping Jesus Christ, Man! Let the rest go.

Today we see profiteers in the Gospel 'business', don't we? Radio preachers who seem to have made a lot of money from their ministries . . .similarly, there are some televangelists who seem to be 'raking it in'. . .but what I hear Paul saying is. . .as long as they are teaching the truth of the Gospel, let the rest go. Oh sure, from my perspective, some of them fall into the 'prosperity gospel' crowd—sometimes peddling that God wants Christians to be materially prosperous—but if others are coming to know Christ from the Scriptures they are teaching, then he will sort the rest out with those preachers. Let it go, Man! Truly, only God can and should judge both the contents and the intent of our hearts.

Keep in mind one thing: God said of his word, "It will not return to me empty, without accomplishing what I desire, and without succeeding in the matter for which I sent it."[2] I view that as a powerful promise actually. It is my part to deliver and share the Word of God; it is the Holy Spirit's part to do the supernatural work in prompting hearts to hear and receive that word, and to show us how to apply it to our lives. It is a marvelous thing when God brings truths from Scripture into our minds, just when needed most. Have you had that happen? You have, if you are a student of his Word, and it is a beautiful thing. Yes, the Word is alive and active, Mr. Hebrews!

And you? Well, you are now free to move about the country, and share the good news!

Grace and Peace,
Christine

1 from 1 Corinthins 9.19ff
2 Isaiah 55.11

From: Christine DiGiacomo <espressocd@cox.net>

Subject: Live or Die, I Win. Philippians 1.19-26

~Remember—because God who called you is faithful.[1]

~Remember—he will not leave you to your own devices; he will never leave you.[2]

~Remember—having faith is a requirement of those who call Jesus 'Lord', for without faith it is impossible to please God.[3]

~Remember—God hears and answers the prayers of the faithful.[4]

~Remember—our lives are meant to glorify God—while we are alive, and through the legacy we leave behind

~Remember—there is joy when believers are in community. There is fellowship, strength, support, love and freedom.[5]

~Remember—we are not citizens of this world, but of Heaven.[6]

It seems that Paul is able to keep these thoughts present in his mind as he writes to the Philippians. He is well aware he might not see them again; he might not see freedom again. In reality, he is aware that he just may be executed—if for no other reason, for preaching a gospel the Romans viewed as subversive to Caesar.

He writes:

~ for I know that through your prayers and the help given by the Spirit of Jesus Christ, what has happened to me will turn out for my deliverance. I eagerly expect and hope that I will in no way be ashamed, but will have sufficient courage so that now as always Christ will be exalted in my body, whether by life or by death. For to me, to live is Christ and to die is gain. If I am to go on living in the body, this will mean fruitful labor for me. Yet what shall I choose? I do not know! I am torn between the two: I desire to depart and be with Christ, which is better by far; but it is more necessary for you that I remain in the body. Convinced of this, I know that I will remain, and I will continue with all of you for your progress and joy in the faith, so that through my being with you again your joy in Christ Jesus will overflow on account of me. Philippians 1.19-26

Do you hear his heart? Do you see his mindset?

"I know that through your prayers and the help given by the Spirit of Jesus Christ . . ." >Paul trusted that his fellow believers were praying for him, and that because of their combined prayers, (his and theirs), he could be expectant of what Christ was going to do in his life, including giving him the courage to accept whatever hand he was dealt—life or death.

". . .so that now as always Christ will be exalted in my body," >from the time Paul came to know Christ, his entire purpose was to honor Jesus Christ. I would like to think that is the way I live my life, but I forget. Some days, I wake up exhausted, stumbling for my caffeinated Peet's elixir, hoping it will help me get school lunches ready on time, books gathered cheerfully, and launched into my own day in an expeditious manner . . .and I forget that my sole purpose is to honor God with my body and mind. Whereas if I had 'honor God in all you do' tattooed on the inside of my eyelids, I would endeavor to do so, even while making school lunches, gathering books, studying Scripture, working out, leading a prayer meeting, etc. Indeed, like Brother Lawrence, I would be mindful to practice the presence of God. "When we are faithful to keep ourselves in his holy presence, and set him always before us, this hinders our offending him, and doing anything that may displease him." . . .Brother Lawrence[7]

"~so that now as always Christ will be exalted. . ." Paul lived to please God. When he was writing to the church at Rome, he waxed eloquent, instructing his Christian brothers to 'offer your bodies as living sacrifices, holy and pleasing to God . . .' How tempting it is to live our lives to please people. 'Tempting?' you say, 'I am enslaved by my own nature, constantly trying to live up to someone else's expectations of me!' Be free, Man. Be free, Woman. Be courageous, and live to honor Christ. What is required of you and me is the same as our brother, Paul—live in such a way "so that now as always Christ will be exalted."

And then the most ironic statement: For to me, to live is Christ and to die is gain. Because it is all about honoring Jesus Christ, to live is to continue to love and serve him; but to die, ah, that is so much better, because then I will be with him! Put simply, Paul is saying, "Live or die, I win . . ."

Grace and Peace,
Christine

1 Thessalonians 5.24
2 Hebrews 13.5
3 Hebrews 11.6
4 James 5.16
5 2 Corinthians 3.17
6 Philippians 3.20
7 from <u>Practicing the Presence of God</u>

From: Christine DiGiacomo <espressocd@cox.net>

Subject: In the face of Persecution . . .
Philippians 1.27-30

Youcef is the pastor of a house church in Rasht, Iran, and was arrested in October 2009 for opposing the education practice that forces non-Muslim students to read the Quran in school. Youcef had argued that the Iranian constitution permits children to be raised in their parents' faith; however, for defying Iranian authorities, Youcef was charged with apostasy.

Iranian officials used pressure tactics during Youcef's imprisonment as an attempt to coerce him to renounce his Christian beliefs, which included arresting his wife and threatening to seize his children. Still, Youcef remained firm in his faith, refusing to deny the name of his Savior Jesus Christ.

On September 22, 2010, Youcef was issued the death sentence for his conversion to Christianity and for encouraging the conversions of other Muslims. Youcef appealed the decision to the Supreme Court of Iran, claiming he had never been a Muslim and therefore could not be found guilty of apostasy. However, a written verdict upholding the death penalty and ordering an investigation was handed down on June 12. A three-day reexamination of the case to determine whether Nadarkhani was a Muslim before his conversion to Christianity proved that Youcef never practiced Islam, but the court decided that he was still guilty of apostasy because his parents were Muslim. Youcef has boldly refused four demands that he recant his faith in Christ and "return" to Islam–making him eligible for execution at any time under Sharia law.[1]

>Dateline: North Korea-

Nowhere in the world is Christian persecution so fierce. Christians have to hide their faith; Christian parents can't even share their beliefs with their children until they are old enough to understand the dangers. Owning a Bible could get you killed, or sent to a harsh labor camp. In 2010 hundreds of Christians were arrested. Some were murdered, others sentenced to labor camps. Despite the risks, the church is growing: there are an estimated 400,000 believers.[2]

In Eritrea, as many as 2,200 believers remain in prison for their faith, while at least 13 have died under the harsh incarceration conditions. It remained very dangerous to be a Christian in Somalia in 2010. At least eight Christians were killed and a quarter of all Christians fled the country. The few Christians are heavily persecuted and must practice their faith in secret. In Nigeria, the forceful implementation of Sharia (Islamic law) in twelve northern states remains a huge challenge for the church. In 2010 there were continued attacks on Christian communities. Extremist Islamic groups, using violence as a means to achieving Muslim dominance, have increased their activities.

I could discuss Afghanistan, Iraq, Yemen, Indonesia, China, and many more countries where it is dangerous to be a Christian, but this will suffice for now. Paul encourages the Philippian believers who are facing, and sure to face more, persecution to stand firm. Take a look:

"Whatever happens, conduct yourselves in a manner worthy of the gospel of Christ. Then, whether I come and see you or only hear about you in my absence, I will know that you stand firm in one spirit, contending as one man for the faith of the gospel without being frightened in any way by those who oppose you. This is a sign to them that they will be destroyed, but that you will be saved—and that by God. For it has been granted to you on behalf of Christ not only to believe on him, but also to suffer for him, since you are going through the same struggle you saw I had, and now hear that I still have." Philippians 1.27-30

What does it mean to conduct ourselves in a manner worthy of the gospel of Christ? To *live* so as to honor the name of Jesus, to *love* so as to draw folks to Christianity, to **subjugate our own needs** for the needs of others, and yes, to **stand strong** in the face of any Christian intolerance.

In the West, it is pretty easy to be a Christian . . .at least for now. So, how should a Christian in the United States 'contend for the faith,' as Paul said? First, know that America is no longer a Christian country; many of our young people have never heard the Gospel of Jesus Christ. In fact, many have been influenced to think that Christians are just ignorant, uninformed, weak people who need a crutch, and perhaps even ought to be pitied. If they have not gotten that message by the time they graduate from their public high school, our colleges will certainly set them straight. The halls of academia are anything but favorable to the cause of Jesus Christ.

How then shall we live? Be aware of the mindsets of the media, popular culture, including the arts, and academia. Understand that a few outspoken, bigoted, hate-filled, and sometimes hypocritical Christians have damaged the cause of Christ. **Know what you believe, and be ready to back it up with solid information**. Scripture says, 'Always be prepared to give an answer to everyone who asks you to give the reason for the hope that you have. But do this with gentleness and respect . . .'[3]

And Christians, pray for your brothers and sisters who are being severely persecuted simply for trying to follow Christ.

Grace and Peace,
Christine

1 Persecution.org
2 Open Doors
3 1 Peter 3.15

From: Christine DiGiacomo <espressocd@cox.net>

Subject: Can you teach us how to grow?

"Can you teach us how to grow in our faith?" Every once in a while a teacher is asked a question that makes her every fiber pop . . .this was just such a question. Hmmm . . .Similarly, I imagine Jesus smiled when the disciples asked him to teach them to pray. 'Now they get it. . .ah yes, now they get it.'

The question 'can you teach us how to grow?' was asked by one of the high school athletes I have just begun leading. As I set to work on the answer, I asked the Lord for direction, for simplicity.

That Sunday night, I had just 30 red New Testaments to spread among almost a hundred students as I asked them to find John chapter 15. (Oh, how I loved watching them turn the pages . . .and yes, I think God himself smiled at the sight) I set the scene for them—Jesus had just shared the Passover meal with his beloved disciples . . .they were in the Upper Room in Jerusalem, while crowds streamed by below. This setting is often referred to as the Last Supper, because Jesus told them that night that he was about to leave them . . .this was the last meal they would share together before Jesus went to the Cross . . .<u>after</u> he had washed their dirty feet like a servant would usually do. . .he told them that one of them was about to betray him. . .he told them that where he was going they could not come—John 13.33. He told them of Heaven, that he was going to prepare a place for them, and they should not be troubled. He promised that when he left them, the Comforter would come . . . and then he said to them, "Come now; let us leave."

And so he leads his best friends down, out of town, and into the vineyard, where he uses the grapevine to symbolize believers' connection with God. "I am the Vine, you are the branches . . .apart from Me, you can do nothing . . ."

On that Sunday night, when we finished reading the few verses, I asked the students three questions: 'what are these verses saying?' Simply, true life comes from being connected to Jesus Christ. 'How does that apply to us?' We must then seek to be connected to him. 'How? Is there any action we should take?' Get to know him through his Word, get to know him by communicating with him——pray. 'Start your day by connecting with the One who made you, the One who knows all about you, the One who loves you.'

And so, before I blow open the first few verses of Philippians chapter two, I invite you to take a look yourself, and ask these same questions: 1) What are the verses saying? What is Paul saying? 2) How do they apply to me? 3) What, if any, action should I take?

"If you have any encouragement from being united with Christ, if any comfort from his love, if any fellowship with the Spirit, if any tenderness and compassion, then make my joy complete by being like-minded, having the same love, being one in spirit and purpose. Do nothing out of selfish ambition or vain conceit, but in humility, consider others better than yourselves. Each of you should look not only to your own interests, but also to the interests of others." Philippians 2.1-4

Give a man a fish; you have fed him for today. Teach a man to fish; and you have fed him for a lifetime. GO ON . . .give it a go . . .what is the passage saying . . .to you? 'Any action you should take? Talk to your Father about it. Grow.

Until the morrow~

Grace and Peace,
Christine

Christine DiGiacomo <espressocd@cox.net>

Going to church is passe. Philippians 2.1

Going to church is passé . . .have you noticed?

Now I am not just talking about 'the world' thinking church is passé, but also God-fearing, God-loving people who have just stopped going to church. However, Friends, we are missing something fundamental to Christianity by doing so. You see, there are certain things that can only be realized by participating in a community of believers who come together for the purpose of worshipping God.

From my youth, I was trained that Christians go to church. That is what we do. Period. I understood the reasons to be quite simple, and I do not think the reasons have changed. First, we are to 'honor the Sabbath, and keep it holy,'[1] which is one of the Ten Commandments. And second, we are to 'not forsake the assembling of ourselves together . . .'[2] (I know I memorized that last verse when I was young because the verbiage is definitely King James!) But let's look at this verse from Hebrews—"Let us not give up meeting together, as some are in the habit of doing, but let us encourage one another—and all the more as you see the Day approaching." So, besides lifting our worship to God, joining together with other believers is meant for our encouragement. In fact, the preceding verse shows that meeting together in the house of God affords us the opportunity to "spur one another on toward love and good deeds."[3]

Christianity is not meant to be either a solo sport or a spectator sport. Let's go back, way back, to the early church, which met in homes in Jerusalem. (ah, so I am not talking about 'church' as it pertains to a building) Why did they come together? First, they had experienced the coming of the Holy Spirit when they had been **together**, waiting in obedience, as Jesus had told them to do. Acts chapter two records that day that changed Christianity forever, and verse 42 highlights the four reasons the believers came together. Followers of Jesus Christ devoted themselves to: the apostles' teaching, and to fellowship, and to sharing meals (including the Lord's Supper), and to prayer.

In Paul's writing to the Philippians, he spurs them on to the unity which can only be had in Jesus Christ . . .

He writes:

"Is there any encouragement from belonging to Christ? Any comfort from his love? Any fellowship together in the Spirit?

Are your hearts tender and compassionate?" Philippians 2.1, New Living Translation

Is there any encouragement from belonging to Christ? Of course there is! **Is there any comfort from his love?** Why, there is no greater comfort than the love of God! **Is there any fellowship together in the Spirit?** Why yes, the world can only offer counterfeit experiences; there is nothing like the people of God being together to share the love of God with one another. It is the Holy Spirit within individual believers that connects the hearts and minds of believers, one with another, and then, ushers in the shared experience of the presence of God, in such a way, that at times, his presence is so real, the feeling so palpable, it cannot be denied. Oh yes, there is fellowship together in the Spirit. **Are your hearts tender and compassionate?** Oh, I pray so. If not, what have you allowed to harden them?

All four of these things should be present and characteristic of the body of believers: **encouragement, comfort, fellowship, and compassion**, for these issue forth from the heart of our loving Father, made possible through the love of Jesus Christ, with the connectivity of the Holy Spirit. These are the shared qualities of faith that we enjoy in a community of believers, and they are indispensable to living as Christians in the world.

Are you discouraged in your faith, or has your ardor waned? Perhaps you have cut yourself off from community . . .or have never experienced it. Does the love of Christ seem more present in someone else's life than your own? Perhaps you need to connect with the people of God. Do you seem to be holding lone Christian beliefs and values in your heart and mind? You will not remain vital without the spark that is present in the people of God. 'Finding yourself a little more cynical, a little less compassionate toward others' needs? You were not meant to be an island, Man. Get in relationship with other Christians—do life together with them.

Let us not give up meeting together, as some are in the habit of doing, but let us encourage one another—and all the more as you see the Day approaching. Indeed, let's spur one another on toward love and good deeds! Church may be passé, but it is definitely not irrelevant, it is vital.

Grace and Peace,
Christine

1 Exodus 20.8; Deuteronomy 5.12
2 Hebrews 10.25
3 Hebrews 10.24

From: Christine DiGiacomo <espressocd@cox.net>

Subject: Danger, Will Robinson! Philippians 2.1-4

I do not really remember much about the television program, but I vividly recall the robot saying, "Danger, Will Robinson . . . Danger!" He swung his arms about as he warned the boy. In a sense, Paul is playing the robot here in Philippians chapter two. 'Warning . . .you may be putting yourselves in jeopardy!'

First, let's get our bearings—Paul went to great lengths to tell the Philippian church of his love and appreciation for their loyalty to him, and their faithfulness to God (in chapter one). Then he reminds them what they have in their body of believers: encouragement, comfort, fellowship, tenderness, mercy and compassion. And then he says, 'make my joy complete by being of the same mind'—which really served as a passionate way of saying, 'stay united'. Take a look:

"If the fact that you are in Christ has any power to influence you, if love has any persuasive power to move you, if you really are sharing in the Holy Spirit, if you can feel compassion and pity, complete my joy, for my desire is that you should be in full agreement, loving the same things, joined together in soul, your minds set on the one thing. Do nothing in a spirit of selfish ambition, and in a search for empty glory, but in humility let each consider the other better than himself. Do not be always concentrating each on your own interests, but let each be equally concerned for the interests of others." Philippians 2.1-4, NRSV

Yes, word had gotten back to Paul that the Philippian community was in danger—it was being threatened from within—by disunity. The danger is of course, as old as man, selfish ambition put ahead of the good of the cause; and in this case, the cause had to be preserved, protected, and revered above anything else—the cause of Christ. But notice with me that at the start, the seeds of disunity often lie in just motives. See, when people are serious about their faith, and their beliefs or convictions really matter to them, then they are apt to come into conflict with others who may see the living out of those beliefs differently. The greater the enthusiasm (or depth of conviction), and the stronger the personalities, the greater potential for disunity that may lead to schisms in the community, which may in turn lead to irreparable disrepair. And then, the cause of Christ is set back, and the Church gets a black eye.

Everyone likes to talk about the 'fruit of the Spirit'—you know, love joy, peace, patience, kindness, goodness, faithfulness, gentleness . . .oh yeah, and <u>self control</u>. . .keeping self under control, Friends.[1] But we must note that before Paul teaches about these, he mentions the 'acts of the flesh', which include, 'discord, selfish ambitions, dissensions, and factions. . .'![2] Not only are these not to have any part in the Christian community, but Paul says 'those who live like this will not inherit the kingdom of God'!

And Jesus? What would Jesus say about disunity in the Church? "By this all men will know that you are my disciples, if you have love for one another."[3] So it would seem that

>disunity in the Christian community does not show the world **love**. It does not bring honor to the name of Jesus Christ. (Now of course, if an individual is departing from Scripture, there must be correction, but we must not divide over 'non-essentials' . . .music styles for worship, tattoos. . . .remember, in the 1960s, hair length for men was a huge issue, now time has given us perspective, and we see how silly that was.)

Paul does not disappoint; within this short passage, he lists five considerations, which, if heeded, should maintain harmony. First, having Christ in common should keep us united. In our desire to honor him, we do all to maintain the bond of peace.

Then, the power of our Christian love should rise above individual differences and selfishness, or 'selfish ambition,' which is an even more apt term. Christian love should seek the good of others before its own, right? True love only comes from God, and it is the highest good we are able to know and realize, this side of Heaven. Godly love is the currency with which we Christians must trade, and it must be preserved ahead of individuality, ahead of the 'almighty self,' which is so esteemed today.

The third unifying truth of Christianity is the presence of the Holy Spirit, which knits believers together, one with another. Elsewhere, Paul told us to 'keep on being filled with the Holy Spirit,'[4] by refraining from sin, staying in the Word, being prayerful, being desirous of the Spirit, and the things of the

Spirit. When believers are filled with the Holy Spirit instead of themselves, there is just not much room for disharmony.

Our Savior was the paragon of compassion, and our Christian community must hold this as one of its distinctives—compassion must be tramped out by disunity.

Finally, Paul appeals to the Philippian believers on a personal note—'make my joy complete by being of the same mind'. Paul's passionate desire for unity to be maintained is the cry of our Lord: 'Child, bring honor to my Father, and be worthy of the name 'Christian' by maintaining unity with one another in the community of Christ. Be one.'

Grace and Peace,
Christine

1 Galatians 5.22-23
2 Galatians 5.19-21
3 John 13.35
4 Ephesians 5.18

From: Christine DiGiacomo <espressocd@cox.net>

Subject: The Church—Love it or Leave it?
Philippians 2.1-4

'In the middle of a messy situation with a church, who represents the church to those who are outside the church?!

Church—what is it to you? No, really. . .stop a moment and think. What is church to you?? We use the word 'church' to describe several different things: There is church, referring to a building; church, meaning worship service—i.e., Did you go to church this morning? From the insiders' perspective, there is 'the church', referring to the Body of Christ around the world, those who profess to follow Jesus; and then from the outsiders' perspective, there is 'the church,' which often refers to 'organized religion', **and** everything that is wrong with it, especially those who come together for various not-so-great reasons. I suppose there may be a fifth category, or at least a sub-category of organized religion—'church', as in the higher-ups in the Vatican, the diocese, 'convention' (if you're Baptist), 'presbytery', (yes, if you're Presbyterian), and so on. So, church: building, worship service, body of Christ, organized religion, and religious governing bodies.

So, what's my messy situation? As you know, I am leading two youth movements, as strange as it is to me. . .still! I mean, ministering in the corporate setting—sure, yah . . .ministering at the bedside of the very ill—sure. . .ministering to a community of women—right on. But this recent thing the Lord is doing still makes me smile. I mean, me, now, high school students? Really, Lord?! ("Movements?" Last Sunday night, when I asked our Varsity football kicker to close our gathering in prayer, as he prayed, he thanked God for 'the movement' taking place in our high school, of people wanting God. Now, how cool is that? How apt!)

Well . . . .a local pastor who has some cool youth-oriented facilities at his church offered to host our "Sunday Night Live." After meeting with the pastor and youth pastor, I said 'hey, we'll try it!' It was really great, because they even served tacos for a hundred kids. Yea, it was great . . .at first. Immediately, there was a 'full court press' for this to be the home of Sunday Night Live, and it was awkward. 'Why, I have the best youth teacher to come along in 30 years and this is a five million dollar facility—all at your disposal!' But it did not feel right.

Two days later, at our weekly leaders' meeting (about 15 students high school students and me), it was unanimous that the team would prefer to meet in private residences, backyards, etc. . . .anything to keep it feeling 'safe' for those who are unfamiliar or ill-at-ease in church. Our goal is to attract students TO Christ. So of course, it was mine to let the pastor know that we were going to keep moving around, (at least for now), and 'we'll talk soon . . .I hope you understand.' Oh, he understood all right, and went around me to the students' Facebook page, lobbying for SNL to meet at his church, and including some offensive comments, like "If anyone thought the sanctuary was too churchy then they are not a Christian . . ." Oh, man . . .then I knew why it had not felt right to me; it wasn't . . .and neither was he. He has continued trying to press his point, with promises of a coffee bar and a shave ice machine, and oh yeah, the best youth speaker he has heard in 30 years. What is he thinking? Does Paul's term 'selfish ambition' fit?

This is the first exposure to 'church' for some of these student leaders, most of whom are about 16 years old. Because they see this fellow as representative of church, what impression do you think will be made on them—with regard to 'the Church'? Oh, and then what about their parents—again, quite a few who do not know God . . .when they hear his inappropriate remarks and his ready judgment of 'outsiders'. . .well, what will they think? And even worse, what will they tell their kids—'See, that's why we don't go to church, Dear. The church is full of guys like him. They are always promoting their own agendas, and oh so judgmental—just like him.'

Unfortunately, the church/Christianity is often marked by select bad experiences had by a small number of people, but the damage is tremendous to the advancement of the Gospel. It is far too easy to lose sight of what Paul wrote: Therefore if you have any encouragement from being united with Christ, if any comfort from his love, if any common sharing in the Spirit, if any tenderness and compassion, then make my joy complete by being like-minded, having the same love, being one in spirit and of one mind. Do nothing out of selfish ambition or vain conceit. Rather, in humility value others above yourselves, not looking to your own interests but each of you to the interests of the others. Philippians 2.1-4

Indeed, presently, there are so many people who have 'had it' with the Church—both the institution and the people—it is tragic. One thing is sure: it breaks the heart of God. The remedy for what is ailing the church is not to leave it—either the brotherhood, the 'body of Christ,' or the coming together for worship—rather, **_we are to love it_**, as Christ loved it and died for it. And also . . .(more to follow)

Grace and Peace,
Christine

From: Christine DiGiacomo <espressocd@cox.net>

Subject: What is the Cure for the Church? (Part two of "The Church—Love it or Leave It?")

Actually, we must approach the answer to that question as Jesus would—what kind of church would Jesus attend, or would he, like so many today, just give up, and leave the church? Hmmm . . .

Since Jesus is the same yesterday, today and forever,[1] then he loves the Church, and he would not leave it—neither Church-the body of believers or Church-the Sabbath worship service. But I do think he might like to shout from a mountain, 'STOP! Take a look at what is being said and done in my name . . .Church, wake up! Rise up and be the people I have called you to be—salt and light in the world.'[2]

In rising up, perhaps then we could see as we ought, from two perspectives: we could see how outsiders view the Church, and also how we might draw professing Christians back to the Church. In both cases, **awareness** of the state of things is necessary. Wake up, believer.

Let's just look at America, which could no longer be called a Christian nation, now could it? The government continues to try to distance itself from the intent of our forefathers, even though our currency says, 'In God we Trust.' Our media portrays Christians as stupid and bigoted because of the rants of a few. Most of academia—public institutions from elementary school through college—espouses an anti-God slant. I have been devouring They Like Jesus, but not the Church,[3] and have found the insights indicative of viewpoints I regularly encounter about Christianity today. Common perceptions of the Church include: The church is an organized religion with a political agenda; it is judgmental and negative; it is arrogant, claiming all other religions are wrong, and it is homophobic. To outsiders, Christians are the Church and the Church is Christians, and we are not seen favorably; we cannot look the other way!

Awareness #1-We live in a post-Christian society
Awareness #2-Christians/the Church not seen favorably

And yet. . .find someone who doesn't like Jesus. . .you would be hard-pressed. From the days he walked the roads of Palestine to today, folks simply cannot deny that he was remarkable in every way. In fact, strike up a casual conversation with someone and ask what he thinks about Jesus . . .most like him. . . .yeah, they do. Most people like Jesus. Even those who have left him.

One of the saddest recollections I have ever read came from a man named Charles Templeton, a preacher who packed the house in the 50s and 60s, (sometimes alongside Billy Graham), but later renounced his faith. Lee Strobel, when doing research for one of his "Case For . . ." books, secured an interview with him when Templeton was into his late 80s and failing quickly. I just feel compelled to share it here:

'Strobel directed the old gentleman's attention to Christ. How would he now assess Jesus at this stage of his life?

Strobel says that, amazingly, Templeton's "body language softened." His voice took on a "melancholy and reflective tone." And then, incredibly, he said:

"He was the greatest human being who has ever lived. He was a moral genius. His ethical sense was unique. He was the intrinsically wisest person that I've ever encountered in my life or in my reading. His commitment was total and led to his own death, much to the detriment of the world."

Strobel quietly commented: "You sound like you really care about him."

"Well, yes," Templeton acknowledged, "he's the most important thing in my life." He stammered: "I . . .I . . .I adore him. . .Everything good I know, everything decent I know, everything pure I know, I learned from Jesus."

Strobel was stunned. He listened in shock. He says that Templeton's voice began to crack. He then said, "I . . .miss . . . him!" With that the old man burst into tears; with shaking frame, he wept bitterly.'[4]

Awareness #3-Most people like and respect Jesus

And for those who have had a relationship with him, if honest, they miss him, just like this poor fellow, Charles Templeton.

A prayer: Lord, in considering a cure for the church today— your church—we Christians must be aware of how we are being perceived. O God, forgive us for not reflecting you well. Show us how to 'be' the Church that attracts outsiders and draws worshippers back—that brings home those who miss you. Show us how to live and love so as to draw people to you . . .for you are life. You alone are love. Amen.

Grace and Peace,
Christine

1 Hebrews 13.8
2 Matthew 5.13.-16
3 a 2007 book by Dan Kimball
4 www.Christian *Courier.com*, 'A Skeptic Reflects on Jesus Christ'
Great resource: *The Case for Faith*, Lee Strobel

The Cure – (Part three behind 'The Church—Love it or Leave It, and "What is the Cure for the Church?")

Jesus was all about truth. He said of himself, "I am the Way, the Truth, and the Life . . ."[1] and "You will know the truth, and the truth will set you free."[2]

So, the ***truth*** is that Christianity has an image problem.

Huh, funny thing, I googled that line, 'Christianity has an image problem', and look what came up:

Photo Illustration by Fred de Noyelle/Godong/Corbis

The top of the first Google offering had this picture—from Time Magazine—which harkens back to yesterday's briefing, in which I said **we should consider what kind of church Jesus would attend** . . .And that Jesus might like to shout at us from a mountain top, 'STOP! Take a look at what is being said and done in my name . . .Church, wake up! Rise up and be the people I have called you to be—salt and light in the world.'

Allow me to connect a few dots here—we need to see Christianity/the Church as it is in today's world. We need to be informed . . .we need to be aware of a few things~

Be aware: this is a post-Christian generation. (more will grow up not knowing Christ than knowing him)
Be aware: Christianity/the Church not viewed favorably
Be aware: In spite of the Church, people still like Jesus

So here it is: the Cure for the Church today is Jesus. Brilliant! The cure for Christianity is for followers of Jesus to be more like him, and less like themselves. As Paul said, we are to do nothing from selfish ambition—Jesus did nothing out of selfish ambition. Jesus was the Man for Others.

Have you ever looked up the definition of 'missionary'? **Missionary – a person sent on a religious mission, one sent to promote Christianity.** That is you. . .that is me. We are alive to promote Jesus; we have no purpose without him. The two previous briefings listed outsiders' viewpoints of the Church, so how might Jesus look at those?

The biggest criticism of the Church today is that She is <u>judgmental</u>. Here's an idea—let's be FOR some things, instead of always AGAINST things. Let's be FOR loving and supporting one another on the 99 things we can agree on, rather than AGAINST the one thing about which we disagree. Let's use judgment in our lives to be judicious with our own words, thoughts and actions; or as my dear mother used to say, why not 'take care of our own red wagon'? And for Pity sake, (who is Pity?), stop sniping at fellow believers if they do not blow their nose the same way you do. I like hankies, you like Kleenex, both suffice—right? Let's stay focused on the essentials of Christianity, and let the rest go.

Now the other side of that coin is that the Church is said to be <u>hypocritical</u>—we say one thing and do another, all the while we are judging someone else. How about this—we will stop being judgmental if you recognize that sometimes we do not mean to be hypocritical . . .I mean sometimes we are trying to uphold the standard, but we fall short—so then should we be judged as hypocritical? Hmmm. . .

And now—allow me, please, to address the accusation that the church is <u>homophobic</u>. I am not sure it is to that extreme, but here's the thing—Christian, you and I do not need to pronounce our judgment on homosexuality; the Bible takes care of that quite nicely. If you are asked, lovingly state what the Bible says; if you are not asked, keep your mouth shut. Believe me, the world knows how Christianity views gays without your two cents; why not throw them off guard, and be like Jesus? Love. Real love draws more people to Jesus than pronouncement of the sin in their lives, can't we see that? Once folks know "love" from us, then our thoughts may mean something to them, our God might mean something, and <u>his</u> views—which are far more important than ours.

Finally, the Church is maligned because it is 'Organized Religion'. Of course, church is organized—God is a God of order! It must be organized; it must be orderly in its function. Critics, say what you mean, rather than hiding behind that euphemism, 'I am against 'organized religion." Do you mean that 'you don't like the church because you see it as a business'? Do you mean that 'you mistrust church leaders because they have hidden behind titles and offices'? Speak plainly. Any church that really lives and loves like Jesus is going to grow from a few relationships to a thriving community; in order to keep that community thriving, it has to be organized. The bummer is when that 'organization' becomes 'religion'—therein lies the problem.

The Cure for what ails the Church is Jesus Christ—knowing him, talking with him, and loving like him. Jesus loved the Church, Jesus loves the Church—you and I are the church, now let's love like it.

1 John 14.6
2 John 8.32 Christianity's Image Problem by David Van Biema, Time Magazine

From: Christine DiGiacomo <espressocd@cox.net>

Subject: Always in context. Philippians 1 through 2.5

Friends, while we look at blocks of Scripture, and apply passages to our lives as well, we must always look at the context of the larger block; hence, take a look at a larger piece of Paul's letter to the Philippians:

This letter is from Paul and Timothy, slaves of Christ Jesus.

I am writing to all of God's holy people in Philippi who belong to Christ Jesus, including the elders and deacons.

May God our Father and the Lord Jesus Christ give you grace and peace.

Every time I think of you, I give thanks to my God. Whenever I pray, I make my requests for all of you with joy, for you have been my partners in spreading the Good News about Christ from the time you first heard it until now. And I am certain that God, who began the good work within you, will continue his work until it is finally finished on the day when Christ Jesus returns.

So it is right that I should feel as I do about all of you, for you have a special place in my heart. You share with me the special favor of God, both in my imprisonment and in defending and confirming the truth of the Good News. God knows how much I love you and long for you with the tender compassion of Christ Jesus.

I pray that your love will overflow more and more, and that you will keep on growing in knowledge and understanding. For I want you to understand what really matters, so that you may live pure and blameless lives until the day of Christ's return. May you always be filled with the fruit of your salvation—the righteous character produced in your life by Christ Jesus—for this will bring much glory and praise to God.

And I want you to know, dear brothers and sisters, that everything that has happened to me here has helped to spread the Good News. For everyone here, including the whole palace guard, knows that I am in chains because of Christ. And because of my imprisonment, most of the believers here have gained confidence and boldly speak God's message without fear.

It's true that some are preaching out of jealousy and rivalry. But others preach about Christ with pure motives. They preach because they love me, for they know I have been appointed to defend the Good News. Those others do not have pure motives as they preach about Christ. They preach with selfish ambition, not sincerely, intending to make my chains more painful to me. But that doesn't matter. Whether their motives are false or genuine, the message about Christ is being preached either way, so I rejoice. And I will continue to rejoice. For I know that as you pray for me and the Spirit of Jesus Christ helps me, this will lead to my deliverance.

For I fully expect and hope that I will never be ashamed, but that I will continue to be bold for Christ, as I have been in the past. And I trust that my life will bring honor to Christ, whether I live or die. For to me, living means living for Christ, and dying is even better. I'm torn between two desires: I would love to go and be with Christ, which would be far better for me. But for your sakes, it is better that I continue to live.

Knowing this, I am convinced that I will remain alive so I can continue to help all of you grow and experience the joy of your faith. And when I come to you again, you will have even more reason to take pride in Christ Jesus because of what he is doing through me.

Above all, you must live as citizens of heaven, conducting yourselves in a manner worthy of the Good News about Christ. Then, whether I come and see you again or only hear about you, I will know that you are standing together with one spirit and one purpose, fighting together for the faith, which is the Good News. Don't be intimidated in any way by your enemies. This will be a sign to them that they are going to be destroyed, but that you are going to be saved, even by God himself. For you have been given not only the privilege of trusting in Christ, but also the privilege of suffering for him. We are in this struggle together. You have seen my struggle in the past, and you know that I am still in the midst of it.

Philippians 2~

Is there any encouragement from belonging to Christ? Any comfort from his love? Any fellowship together in the Spirit? Are your hearts tender and compassionate? Then make me truly happy by agreeing wholeheartedly with each other, loving one another, and working together with one mind and purpose.

Don't be selfish; don't try to impress others. Be humble, thinking of others as better than yourselves. Don't look out only for your own interests, but take an interest in others, too.

You must have the same attitude that Christ Jesus had. vv. 1-5

Next, we will consider Jesus Christ . . .who is he? Who was he?

Grace and Peace,
Christine

From: Christine DiGiacomo <espressocd@cox.net>

Subject: Who IS Jesus Christ?
(set up for Philippians 2.5-8)

I can see their two beautiful young faces so clearly in my mind . . .one is dark, the other is light; one has a strong football build, the other a tall, lean volleyball build; one has grown up in a Hindu household, the other just a family who didn't talk too much about God, didn't believe in church either. Both young men were there that cold, windy Easter day when I baptized their friend at a local beach. Both attend Fellowship of Christian Athletes and Sunday Night Live; actually, they don't miss a meeting, and even show up to the leaders' meetings too. . .it seems they do not want to miss anything, especially when it comes to filling in the blanks about Christianity.

They have heard several personal God stories, and they are now ready to really entertain the question: Who is this Jesus Christ people are talking about? Who is Jesus Christ? The blonde one said, 'No, who <u>was</u> Jesus Christ?' See, he wants to hear about Jesus' life on earth—he did not grow up hearing the stories of Jesus.

And so I sat down with pen and paper . . .The question itself is a tricky one—'Who is Jesus?' But if you are not a believer yet, perhaps you need to start with the question, 'Who was Jesus?' Why would Jesus come to earth with the express purpose of dying?

The further I go into a position piece about Jesus, maybe it becomes 'Why Christianity?' rather than 'Who is Jesus?' I guess these questions are two sides of the same coin. To study the life of this sinless human being is to realize there is something far greater at work than just coming up with satisfactory answers; and that something is critically important.

So, who WAS Jesus? He was begotten, not made. He already existed, has always been, along with God the Father and the Holy Spirit. At the right time in history, Jesus willingly took on the flesh of a Jewish baby, born to royalty as befitting a King . . .NO! Jesus was born to a peasant maiden, a virgin, from a back country town, Nazareth.

Jesus was born in satin-y splendor with many attending he and his young mother—with her own mother, mopping her brow and holding her hand . . .NO! 'Born far from little Nazareth, away from Mary's home, without the help of her mother . . .at a time when the census workers did not go door to door, but when all had to go to the city of their lineage to register. For Mary's betrothed, Joseph, that meant traveling to Bethlehem, because he was of the line of King David. It was at least a three-day trip from Nazareth, at a time when Mary was close to delivering her holy child.

We do not know much about Jesus' childhood, though we know that Mary and Joseph knew the Messiah was growing up in their home, eating at their table. They raised Jesus like other Jewish children, steeped in the Scriptures, the religious observances and feasts, and equipped him in Joseph's carpentry trade.

Jesus began his ministry at the age of 30, recruiting 12 men to work alongside; he would mature and mentor them, and one day, leave his work for them to take to the world. The disciples looked on as Jesus taught of his father and of the kingdom, which would have no end. They watched as Jesus broke the social mores of his day, extending himself to a Samaritan—reviled and hated by his people—to women, who were viewed as second-class citizens at best—to children, who he loved and embraced. He offended the pious Pharisaical Jews healing on the Sabbath; he broke the laws of nature by working miracles, casting out demons, and restoring sight to the blind. Neither the Jewish teachers nor the Roman leaders could figure him out, and they certainly could not contain him. Jesus was at home with sinners and people of ill repute, dining with crooked tax collectors and loose women. His love drew them to holiness, as he modeled a better way, taught by example in word and in deed.

Jesus knew his strength lie in his connection with his father, so he met alone to pray, to connect, and to seek direction. He said and did only what his father had him do; he did not execute his own will, but rather his father's plan and purposes.

Ultimately, he allowed himself to suffer and die, without defending himself . . .for you, for me.

There's more—yes, there's so much more, so stay with me, won't you?

Grace and Peace,
Christine

From: Christine DiGiacomo <espressocd@cox.net>

Subject: Jesus Christ, lost without him.
(set-up for Philippians 2.5-11)

Unless you are in contact with the young public, you really do not have a framework for the claim that 'we live in a Post-Christian generation'—that more people will grow up <u>not</u> knowing about Jesus Christ than will. I recently addressed the feeling of many that the Church is so flawed they want no part of it. In fact, parents, thinking themselves generous, tell their teen-agers, 'hey, be glad—I am not dragging you to a boring church service, or forcing my beliefs on you. I am letting you make up your own mind.' 'Sounds magnanimous but today's teens NEED God—maybe more than any generation before—there is so much pressure. There is so much thrown at them, and they need biblical training to make wise decisions.

This weekend, I asked a local youth pastor to come and speak at Sunday Night Live, and answer the question, "Who is Jesus Christ?" In order to illustrate the heart of Jesus, he went to Luke chapter 15, and the story of the Prodigal Son; he asked, 'how many of you know this story?' In a crowd of just under a hundred students, three hands went up. Three.

It seems our culture welcomes any "ism", ideology, or religion other than biblical Christianity. Our young people have lost out, I'm afraid. 'Interesting that on April 6, 2009, President Obama was in Turkey, a Muslim country, and said, "We do not consider ourselves a Christian nation."[1] No kidding, Mr. Obama . . .and thank you very much. Quite telling.

In "Who IS Jesus Christ?" I discussed the Son of God, and who he WAS when he came in the flesh. Just digging into my own head and heart to answer that question, 'Who is Jesus?' reminded me why I love him so. Perhaps the most remarkable thing about Jesus' 33-plus year stay is that he came to earth for one purpose—to die. Yet, he came . . .knowing the torture that would be his.

Yes, ultimately, he allowed himself to suffer and die in the most humiliating and excruciating form of execution known to man. And he died without defending himself . . .for you, for me.

Death, of course, could not contain Jesus! The tomb was found empty, and the boulder that blocked its entrance, estimated between 1½ and two tons, had been rolled uphill and away from the tomb. Death could not contain Jesus nor could the tomb, or the Roman guard unit stationed there. Those Roman guards were strictly disciplined fighting men held to the highest standards. Failure often required death by torturous and humiliating methods. The massive stone had the Roman seal affixed to it, which stood for the power and authority of the Roman Empire. Breaking the seal meant automatic execution by crucifixion—upside down.[2] Anyone trying to move the stone from the tomb's entrance would have broken the seal and thus incurred the wrath of Roman law.

No matter. Jesus rose from the dead on the third day, just as he said he would. For 40 days, he walked, talked and even ate with people; he met them face-to-face, individually and in groups, indoors and out of doors, when he preached to a crowd of more than 500. And then from the Mount of Olives, Jesus Christ, before the very eyes of his beloved disciples and several others, ascended into Heaven to assume his rightful place with God the Father.

Who is Jesus? He is the beautiful Son of God; he is our Savior, and our access to God. Jesus is in every way God. He lives to intercede to the Father on our behalf.[3]

Who IS Jesus? Savior, Teacher, coming King, Lord, Friend, Shepherd, Miracle-worker. He is compassionate, merciful, an extender of Grace, and our holy Lord.

Who WILL Jesus BE? Our King, and the Judge of the living and the dead.[3]

Who IS he? Who WAS he? Who WILL he be? Well . . .

>God is outside of time and space . . .Therefore,
   Jesus IS all of these at once—Creator,
       Miracle-worker, Teacher, Suffering Savior,
       Conqueror of Death, Coming King.

Check it out: http://www.youtube.com/watch?v=upGCMl_bOn4

Jesus Christ—My life would be empty without him, and I would have no purpose and no barometer. Jesus Christ, lost without him.

Grace and Peace,
Christine

Sources:
1. public record—even on Youtube
2. <u>Riverpower.org</u>
3. Hebrews 7.25
4. 1 Peter 4.5
5. Psalm 33.9; Colossians 1.16

From: Christine DiGiacomo <espressocd@cox.net>

Subject: One of these things is not like the other. . .or is it? Philippians 2.5-8

Did you ever have preschoolers who watched Sesame Street? There were these little dramatic sketches where viewers would be shown a group of four items, one of which was different from the other three, and they would have to identify the item that didn't belong . . .like here in Philippians 2—which doesn't belong? human, humbled, servant, God. Which of the four does not belong? God. Unless or until Jesus Christ . . . right? Let's take a look:

Paul charged the Philippians with being more concerned about others than themselves, of spurning selfishness and conceit, and choosing instead to be like Jesus: Your attitude should be the same as that of Christ Jesus: Who, being in very nature God, did not consider equality with God something to be grasped, but made himself nothing, taking the very nature of a servant, being made in human likeness. And being found in appearance as a man, he humbled himself and became obedient to death—even death on a cross!

Here is what we have: Jesus Christ – in nature God, equal with God. And yet . .Jesus Christ chose to make himself <u>nothing</u>, assumed the nature of a <u>servant</u>, took on human flesh, <u>humbled</u> himself, chose to be <u>obedient</u>, even to death—to the worst kind of death, crucifixion.

Have this attitude in yourselves which was also in Christ Jesus->humility. Humility isn't something regarded too highly in our culture, however the Scriptures hold out humility as a virtue to be sought after, a quality to embody, a discipline to be practiced and honed, an attitude to possess. 'Interesting to hold this disposition of humility up against the perception of The Church today, which we have just discussed—judgmental, hypocritical, homophobic, etc.—'seems we Christians (insiders) need to examine ourselves, so that outsiders see The Church as more like Jesus—humble, unselfish, and not self-seeking. It is clear that God puts a premium on humility, while he despises the kind of pride that stems from self-righteousness. God hates anything that creates a hindrance to seeking him.

Scripture is quite clear on this humility thing—"What does the Lord require of you? To act justly and to love mercy and to walk humbly with your God."[1] Are you humble? It certainly influences your attitude about life, you know. If you operate from a correct view of yourself, it means you look through lenses of humility. Humility >holds the feelings of others dear, >rightly values God-esteem above all else, and >fights the natural human bent of self-centeredness.

Wanting to be humble, a man isn't thinking just about how 'this or that' makes him feel, or 'what's in it' for him—no, he is not thinking just of himself, but rather the needs of others before his own.

"Lord, show us how to be humble."

Humility gives us right perspective in our relationships—vertical and horizontal. To be clear, I am not suggesting that being humble means being self-effacing or self-deprecating. Note to self: when we are self-effacing or self-deprecating we may just be exhibiting different forms of pride that turn voices of reassurance our way. Humility is not putting ourselves down, it is not lousy self esteem or lack of confidence; rather, True humility comes from a place of strength and inner security. **In order to truly be secure within, we must know *Whose we are*, and therefore, *Who we are*.** Genuinely humble people who have a desire to seek the well-being of others are generally very secure people. They are fully aware of their gifts, their training, their experience, and all the attributes that make them successful at whatever they do. That security—that honest, healthy self-assessment—results in more than healthy self-assessment—results in more than a humble constitution. It translates into actions that can be observed, actions that we want to emulate, and actions that reflect favorably on Jesus Christ.[2] (and "The Church")

Humility is a right position of the heart—toward the Lord, toward others, and ourselves. That right heart position takes things that don't seem like the other, and makes them qualities of the other: Christian—servant, unselfish, un-assuming, and self-sacrificing. One of these things may not seem like the other, but really, it is what we are called to be!

Grace and Peace,
Christine

1 Micah 6.8
2 Partial thoughts from Chuck Swindoll, So, You Want to be Like Christ?

From: Christine DiGiacomo <espressocd@cox.net>

Subject: The Crux of the Matter. Philippians 2.9-11

Crux – (noun) 1. A vital or pivotal point, 2. A turning point, 3. An intersection of people or ideas, 4. An issue that is ongoing or unresolved, 5. A cross (Latin for cross)

Today's passage is the crux of the New Testament . . .I might even be so bold as to say that it is the crux of the Bible, and the heart of God.

Therefore because Jesus humbled himself, became a man, and died—sinless—in our place . . .**God exalted him to the highest place and gave him the name that is above every name, that *at the name of Jesus every knee should bow, in heaven and on earth and under the earth, and every tongue confess that Jesus Christ is Lord, to the glory of God the Father.*** Philippians 2.9-11

We have been discussing Jesus' life and purpose; we saw what Paul said, have this attitude in yourself which was also in Christ Jesus: humility. Jesus Christ—fully God, fully human, and humble? Hmm . . .I am wondering, if someone turned to you on the airplane and said, 'I see the cross around your neck. . .um, could you tell me about Jesus Christ?' Could you?

Let's say you had your son's friend for dinner at your house . . .you just said 'the blessing' and then, "In Jesus' name, Amen. . ." Your son's friend lifts his head to say, 'Um, excuse me, Mrs. Weld, could you tell me about Jesus? Um, you prayed 'in Jesus' name', could you tell me about him?' Well, Mrs. Weld, could you do it? Could you tell your son's friend, or anyone else who asked, about Jesus? Could you, through your expressive words, capture the essence of Jesus Christ?

It matters, you know. From today's passage we see that just any understanding of Jesus will not do. . .it is not enough to say that 'Jesus was a good and moral individual;' it is not sufficient to say that 'Jesus was the best teacher the world has known. . .' no, only one description of Jesus is sufficient. **Jesus is Lord.** As Paul expressed to the Philippians, you and I must believe, must be willing to speak aloud that "Jesus Christ is Lord of All . . .Jesus Christ is the Lord of my life." Jesus himself said, 'Everyone who acknowledges me publicly here on earth, I will also acknowledge before my Father in heaven."[1] Yep, we must be willing to claim him.

Which reminds me—when Jesus said, 'Not everyone who says to me, 'Lord, Lord,' will enter the kingdom of heaven, but only he who does the will of my Father who is in heaven,'[2] What did he mean? What did Jesus mean 'that not everyone who says 'Lord, Lord' will enter the kingdom of heaven, but only he who does the will of my Father'? Let's look at the context, here in Matthew 7—verse 20 indicates that it was those who bear fruit—those whose lives exhibit that they are connected to the Vine, Jesus Christ.

For you to say "Jesus is Lord" means that you are in a sweet surrendered relationship to him; indeed, it means that I have subjugated my will to his will, to his way of looking at things, to his way of doing things. It means that you and I have determined to rest our case with him.

These few verses also proclaim the position of God the Father—that one day, ALL will bow, ALL will recognize that Jesus Christ is the Lord Supreme. Our Father will smile. Jesus IS Lord of all—that is the crux of the matter.

Grace and peace,
Christine

1 Matthew 10.32
2 Matthew 7.21

From: Christine DiGiacomo <espressocd@cox.net>

Subject: Are you a healthy tree?

Are you a healthy tree? Philippians 2.12-13

City folk like to plant lemon trees somewhere in their yards—have you noticed? In my area, olive trees have been en vogue for a while, too. And while I grew up in a coastal California town, my family often drove through rich farmland, on our way to visit both my mother and my dad's kin. As we drove through the Central Valley, Mom and Dad would name the various crops and orchards—avocados, apricots, walnuts, almonds, and of course, a lot of orange groves. Yes, they could identify the trees by their fruit; and often, even when the trees were not in season, they knew by their growth pattern, leaves, and even irrigation. What does that have to do with you and me? Nothing . . . unless we are disciples of Jesus.

Dear friends, you always followed my instructions when I was with you. And now that I am away, it is even more important. Work hard to show the results of your salvation, obeying God with deep reverence and fear. For God is working in you, giving you the desire and the power to do what pleases him. Philippians 2.12-13

Therefore—because Jesus humbled himself, became a man, and died for us, and because he is Lord of all—you and I ought to continue to pursue an understanding of what it means to be like Christ, and follow him in obedience. BUT WAIT . . . does that mean it is all up to us? That if we do not <u>do enough</u>, we just might find ourselves on the outside looking in? And then . . .what is enough?

From across a large room yesterday, one of my Bible study sisters bravely admitted, 'this scares me. What if I am not doing the right things and he rejects me one day?' Huh, well in light of Jesus' words, 'Not everyone who says to me, 'Lord, Lord,' will enter the kingdom of heaven, but only he who does the will of my Father who is in heaven,[1]' I can understand her dismay. Another dear sister in high emotion blurted out, 'I even know the right things to do, but I am so overwhelmed with homeschooling my two children and life in general, I am afraid Jesus might say, 'depart from Me, I never knew you'! How can I be sure? Truthfully, I'm terrified!'

These were serious questions; they were good and right questions, and yes, the discussion is another reason why Christians are 'not to forsake the assembling of themselves together[2]'. The writer of Ecclesiastes said, 'a cord of three strands is not easily broken[3]'. In this case, I had already been engaged in the mental gymnastics of what Paul was talking about, that Jesus must be Lord. . .and that Jesus said, not all who say 'lord, lord' will enter Heaven. . .plus, I knew what was coming, right here in Philippians 2. Look what Paul says above—"it is God who works in you".

Decision. Commitment. Discipline. Fruit. ~ It is a process.

I believe that 'doing the will of the Father' starts with a decision to follow Jesus Christ, and a commitment to 'do what it takes', to obey him. We only know what to obey by reading the Word, and communing with God in prayer. Both require discipline—when we are in his Word and practice prayer, we are abiding in Jesus Christ. When we abide in Jesus Christ, we cannot help but bear fruit. That is the process of transformation—the morphing of ourselves into an individual who follows the heartbeat of Jesus.

Now, read again Paul's words: "Work hard to show the results of your salvation, obeying God with deep reverence and fear. For God is working in you, giving you the desire and the power to do what pleases him."

Let's go back to my two sisters—do they have cause to fear that they will be rejected? God is looking—God always looks—at our hearts. Both have the Spirit of God residing within, both desire to please their Father . . .both are 'in process'. If they continue to cooperate with God in the process (sanctification), HE will do it. . .HE will transform them. . .HE will cause them to be trees firmly planted, with roots going down deep, and much fruit being produced.

Are you a healthy tree? If you do not see any fruit hanging from your branches, perhaps you are not. Check the process above . . .has your commitment to him flagged? Have you gotten away from the discipline of the Word, away from communicating with the Lover of your soul? If so, turn around . . .where are you stuck? And then ask God to grow your desire for him, for his Word, for growth, and to be fruitful . . .he will grant you your request. It is a prayer he is dying to answer; actually, he already did.

Grace and Peace,
Christine

1) Matthew 7.21
2) Hebrews 10.25
3) Ecclesiastes 4.12

From: Christine DiGiacomo <espressocd@cox.net>

Subject: Stars in Training. Philippians 2.14-16

Where do people go to wax philosophic these days? From my days in and around university coffee shops, I remember them as rich with lively debate—sometimes on important life issues, sometimes over hotly-debated minutia of some academic matter, but always, tables of folks locked in intense discussion. In the first-century Greek cities to which Paul traveled, it was gymnasiums that drew philosophers and sophists, wandering teachers and preachers . . .each drawing their own kinds of audiences. Socrates could often be found in the gymnasium discussing questions about eternity. The Greek word 'gymnasion' referred to a place where both physical and intellectual training of young men took place; for the Greeks, there was as much emphasis on athletic training as intellectual. Several places in Paul's writing, he used the athlete's training and goals as symbolic for spiritual training.

"I beat my body and make it my slave,"[1] he said, comparing his personal spiritual discipline to that of the boxer or wrestler. ***"I continue my pursuit toward the goal, the prize of God's upward calling, in Christ Jesus."***[2] "Do you not know that the runners in the stadium all run in the race, but only one wins the prize? Run so as to win. Every athlete exercises discipline in every way."[3]

Remember—this was the day of the ancient games. When we studied Paul's letters to the church at Corinth, (Corinthians), he referenced winning a wreath that perishes vs. an imperishable crown . . .in reference to the Isthmian games. Then there were the Pan-Ionian games at Ephesus, and the greatest of them all—the Olympian games. The athletes came from far and wide, but right along with them were the historians, poets, and even sculptors, who on location, formed clay into statues of the winners. (I find that fascinating!)

There is no question but that Paul was a spectator at these games, so familiar was he with the contests, and the brilliant parallels to the life of an authentic follower of Jesus Christ. "Discipline" was a beautiful thing to Brother Paul; he demanded it of himself, and taught us that God requires it of his children. Take a look:

Do everything without complaining or arguing, so that you may become blameless and pure, children of God without fault in a crooked and depraved generation, in which you shine like stars in the universe as you hold out the word of life—in order that I may boast on the day of Christ that I did not run or labor for nothing.

Complaining/Arguing should not be part of the Christian's "M.O.". The mindset of the malcontent does not represent Christ well; it keeps us from being what we are called to be—blameless and pure—"children of God without fault in a crooked and depraved generation". Huh, if the world seemed crooked and depraved to Paul in the first century, how would he describe this generation? Yet we are still called to purity, we are still called to righteousness, because he who called us is holy, and it is he who sets the standard. We are to 'shine like stars in the universe . . .' Paul said. Stars shine at night, stars stand out in the night, stars provide light, and stars point people home.

Paul links the Philippian Christians' steadfast behavior with his own finish; and on the Day of Judgment, it matters to Paul to finish well. He does not want to just limp across the Finish Line . . .he wants to run, all out, with all his energy expended for the cause of Christ, crossing the finish line, breaking the tape with his chest lifted high. That's a great finish!

Grace and Peace,
Christine

1 1 Corinthians 9.27
2 Philippians 3.14
3 1 Corinthians 9.24, 25

From: Christine DiGiacomo <espressocd@cox.net>

Subject: Sacrifice? Huh? Philippians 2.14-18

There was brilliance in the simplicity of Jesus' parables, as he used familiar pastoral terms to make his teaching come alive for his first century listeners. And when Paul compared the active life of Christian faith to athletic training, we can easily visualize the disciplined life of an athlete, and even relate to it. However, when Paul refers to himself 'being poured out as a drink offering,' few, if any of us, have any context for that. So, do we skip over it or seek to understand it?

Take a look:

Do all things without complaining and disputing, that you may become blameless and harmless, children of God without fault in the midst of a crooked and perverse generation, among whom you shine as lights in the world, holding fast the word of life, so that I may rejoice in the day of Christ that I have not run in vain or labored in vain. Yes, and if I am being poured out *as a drink offering* on the sacrifice and service of your faith, I am glad and rejoice with you all. For the same reason you also be glad and rejoice with me. **Philippians 2:14-18,** New King James Version (NKJV)

Whatever could he mean by the term 'drink offering'? First, let me remind us that he was writing a letter to the Philippian church whom he loved. First and foremost, he wrote so that they could understand—I mean, let's get serious—Paul did not know as he was writing, that 2,000 years later a very modern, industrialized, global readership of varied languages and cultures would be reading and gleaning from this letter! (However, God knew—and remember, 'all Scripture was inspired by God'[1]; it was God-breathed into the heart and mind of the writer of Scripture) So, the Philippians to whom Paul was writing knew what he meant by 'being poured out as a drink offering on the sacrifice and service of your faith' . . .for us, some historical contextual digging is then in order.

One of the most common kinds of sacrifice in Greek and Roman religion was a libation, which was a cup of wine poured out as an offering to the gods.[2] For instance, for non-Christians, every meal began and ended with such a libation, as a kind of grace before and after food. Ah . . . so, back to Paul's writing—he is saying that he looks at the faith and service of the Philippians as a sacrifice to God.

In addition, (remember that Paul writes from prison, awaiting trial, aware that he may be executed by the Romans). . .he says he is ready and willing to be a sacrifice to God himself.

With that in mind, in essence, Paul is saying to his beloved Philippians brothers, 'your Christian fidelity and loyalty are already a sacrifice to God; and if death for Christ should come to me, then I am willing and glad that my life should be poured out like a libation on the altar of which your sacrifice is being made.' And look back at the text . . .if that should happen—"if I am being poured out *as a drink offering* on the sacrifice and service of your faith, I am glad and rejoice with you all. For the same reason you also be glad and rejoice with me"—indeed, if I am martyred, my friends, rejoice with me. Wow, that is incredible.

What are you and I called to sacrifice for Jesus Christ? It will not be the libation of wine that Paul's first-century readers would have understood . . .for some of you reading this, though—in China, India, Pakistan, Nigeria, Eritrea, where Christianity is punishable by law—like Paul, your life may be required of you.

But for readers in the West, I challenge you to consider what this passage means to you—what sort of sacrifice might God require of you?

For starters, *"live a life of love, just as Christ loved us and gave himself up for us as a fragrant offering and sacrifice to God."*[3] And too, perhaps we are to look at the area of sanctification—where God works his transforming power in our lives—and ask him to look at areas where compromise has sneaked in . . .Have you and I become too permissive with ourselves, exercising 'Christian liberty' just a little too liberally? Here, I will go first . . .yes, I have.

Grace to you. . .grace to me,
Christine

1 2 Timothy 3.16
2 William Barclay, *The Letters to the Philippians, Colossians, and Thessalonians*
3 Ephesians 5.2

From: Christine DiGiacomo <espressocd@cox.net>

Subject: Paul's love for Timothy.

Have you ever read someone else's letter? Of course, you have. Entire books of letters by noteworthy folks are best-sellers . . .why? They give us insight as to the individuals' thinking and heart.

Paul's letter (closing out Philippians 2), moves from discussing proper Christian conduct, including the importance of maintaining unity and being humble, to what appears to be some 'housekeeping' business.

"I hope in the Lord Jesus to send Timothy to you soon, that I also may be cheered when I receive news about you. I have no one else like him, who will show genuine concern for your welfare. For everyone looks out for their own interests, not those of Jesus Christ. But you know that Timothy has proved himself, because as a son with his father he has served with me in the work of the gospel. I hope, therefore, to send him as soon as I see how things go with me. And I am confident in the Lord that I myself will come soon." verses 19-24

Paul's keen love and appreciation for Timothy are obvious. There was no one as close to Paul as Timothy. It seems that the two men met on Paul's first missionary journey, when Timothy was just a teen-ager. Paul recognized something keen in Timothy; in fact, in his letter to the church at Corinth, he referred to Timothy as 'his beloved son'. Indeed he was much like a spiritual son to Paul. As Paul writes from prison in Rome, it is Timothy who is taking care of his needs, yet Paul is willing to selflessly send him back to the Philippians to serve them—which of course is illustrative of Paul's heart for the church, and his great love for them. (Imagine being a representative of Paul—that he might have that great kind of faith in you! Paul had great confidence in Timothy.)

Paul said of his spiritual son, 'I have no one else like him, who will show genuine concern for your welfare.' Timothy saw the vision of Jesus Christ in Paul's eyes. . .he understood it, and was willing to do whatever he could to serve Jesus by serving Paul. Second place was just fine with Timothy. I have a "Timothy", but her name is Lisa. Like Timothy, for about five years now, Lisa knew the vision I have for serving Jesus Christ, and she has been willing to serve alongside me—and even serve me personally—because she knows in doing so, it is the Lord Jesus Christ she is serving.

While Paul does not elaborate on the nature of Timothy's spiritual gifts, there is no doubt that Timothy's gifts were well suited to work with Paul's gifts of teaching, evangelism, and shepherding. Lisa's gifts of administration, discernment, encouragement, shepherding, and faith work hand-in-glove with my gifts. When the Lord led me to establish a non-profit so that the work of the gospel could go 'global' as the Lord had instructed, it was Lisa who helped me process the paperwork with Legalzoom, since I could not afford an attorney to handle the legal documents. No task has been too small, but no task has ever been too big either. She researches for me sometimes, she sets me up in technology she would love to have but can't afford, and then teaches me how to use it. At the last women's retreat where I spoke, she went with me, and sat in the audience and prayed for all of the women, and for me. And now, when ministry demands more of me than I have to go around, Lisa ministers to the women in our Bible study, ably loving them and helping them during life's great storms—all the while, I can trust what she says, trust how she counsels, knowing that as Paul said of Timothy, "I have no one else like HER, who will show genuine concern for your welfare. For everyone looks out for their own interests, not those of Jesus Christ."

One day, when I am in Heaven, and my children are reading my letters and writings, they will understand the value of ministering with a partner who loves God and serves him faithfully by serving others . . .and is willing to serve alongside them to make God's vision come to pass. Thank you, Timothy; thank you, Lisa. I love you.

p.s. If you are leading a ministry alone, pray for a Timothy.

Grace and Peace,
Christine

From: Christine DiGiacomo <espressocd@cox.net>

Subject: Some thoughts to ponder from Philippians . . .

Some Philippians thoughts thus far . . .

Grace and peace to you from God our Father and the Lord Jesus Christ. **Words to live by from Philippians 1:** [I am] confident of this, that he who began a good work in you will carry it on to completion until the day of Christ Jesus. >*For whom are you praying? Have they 'lost their first love of Jesus Christ'? Do not lose heart, my dear friends.*

And this is my prayer: that your love may abound more and more in knowledge and depth of insight, so that you may be able to discern what is best and may be pure and blameless until the day of Christ, filled with the fruit of righteousness that comes through Jesus Christ—to the glory and praise of God. For to me, to live is Christ and to die is gain. >*Either way, I win.*

Whatever happens, conduct yourselves in a manner worthy of the gospel of Christ. >*Note to self: is my conduct worthy of Jesus?*

Words to live by from Philippians 2: If you have any encouragement from being united with Christ, if any comfort from his love, if any fellowship with the Spirit, if any tenderness and compassion, then make my joy complete by being like-minded, having the same love, being one in spirit and purpose. >*Unity in the body of Christ is imperative! The world is watching.*

Do nothing out of selfish ambition or vain conceit, but in humility consider others better than yourselves. Each of you should look not only to your own interests, but also to the interests of others. >*Consider the feelings of others first.*

Your attitude should be the same as that of Christ Jesus: >humble!

Who, being in very nature God, did not consider equality with God something to be grasped, but made himself nothing, taking the very nature of a servant, being made in human likeness. And being found in appearance as a man, he humbled himself and became obedient to death—even death on a cross!

Therefore God exalted him to the highest place and gave him the name that is above every name, that at the name of Jesus every knee should bow, in heaven and on earth and under the earth, and every tongue confess that Jesus Christ is Lord, to the glory of God the Father.

Therefore, my dear friends, as you have always obeyed—not only in my presence, but now much more in my absence—continue to work out your salvation with fear and trembling, for it is God who works in you to will and to act according to his good purpose. *>Press in . . .press on—discipline yourself to pursue what it means to honor Christ, what it means to be transformed; and then, participate with the Holy Spirit within you—as you morph into a more Christ-like person.*

Do everything without complaining or arguing, *>Wow! This is what Paul highlights to indicate that we are becoming pure Christians? You mean there is that much wrong with complaining and arguing? Hmmm . . . I think this might take us back to pursuing humility, maintaining unity, and thinking of others' feelings before our own.*

. . .so that you may become blameless and pure, children of God without fault in a crooked and depraved generation, in which you shine like stars in the universe. . .

'Thankful for Paul's relationship with the Philippians, 'thankful that he wrote to them, 'thankful that I can glean from the table.

Grace and Peace,
Christine

From: Christine DiGiacomo <espressocd@cox.net>

Subject: Commendation = Encouragement. Philippians 2.25-30

It is difficult to navigate his name: E-pa-phro-di-tus . . .and why bother? It seems as though Paul is just addressing a house-keeping matter—sending him back to the church in Philippi. The point seems superfluous in this magnificent chapter two of Philippians, so rich with teaching about the body of Christ. When Paul talks about the importance of humility, saying we ought have the same disposition as Jesus Christ, who gave up his place next to God the Father to take on the body of a man . . .all to suffer and die. . .and then, 'oh yeah, Boys, in addition, I am sending Epaproditus back to you . . .'! What is the point?

Well, first remember in the preceding few verses Paul has mentioned Timothy, that he will send him back to them soon, but is still in need of his ministry—then took the opportunity to commend Timothy, and indicate what he has meant to him. Indirectly, we see Paul's humility in sharing the work of the Gospel with another Christian brother—Timothy—though he was much more like a spiritual son to Paul than a brother. It takes nothing away from Paul to give value to another fellow laborer in the cause of Christ. Indeed it is important to give credit where credit is due. Just think how much that commendation must have meant to Timothy!

He writes: "But I think it is necessary to send back to you Epaphroditus, my brother, fellow worker and fellow soldier, who is also your messenger, whom you sent to take care of my needs. For he longs for all of you and is distressed because you heard he was ill. Indeed he was ill, and almost died. But God had mercy on him, and not on him only but also on me, to spare me sorrow upon sorrow. Therefore I am all the more eager to send him, so that when you see him again you may be glad and I may have less anxiety. Welcome him in the Lord with great joy, and honor men like him, because he almost died for the work of Christ, risking his life to make up for the help you could not give me." Philippians 2.25-30

'See how he loved them!' Paul was bold in expressing his feelings for the two men who had come to minister alongside him. Our Lord was like that—Jesus was 'out there' with how he loved; I think of when Lazarus died. He arrived on the scene to find Lazarus' sisters, Mary and Martha, so distraught over their brother's passing, that it moved him to tears—yea, not just tears, but his good friend said, "Jesus wept.[1]" Jesus was a man of great compassion, and courageous enough to let people see his heart. Similarly, we see Paul's heart right here in the end of Philippians 2. In Paul's note about Epaphroditus, he expresses several things—compassion, validation and blessing, and also good business sense.

The Philippian believers had sent Epaphroditus to Paul, bearing a monetary gift and the task of seeing to Paul's needs. Unfortunately, he got very sick, and it was best he return home. Paul commends him as a 'brother, fellow worker and fellow soldier,' thereby imbuing him with significance. 'Messenger, care-giver, and now needing to be cared for himself,' Paul intimates about Epaphroditus; 'receive him and honor him,' are Paul's words.

Paul honors both Timothy and Epaphroditus by commending them for their ministry. In your life and in mine, **who do we need to commend**? Who do we need to recognize and pay honor with our words? When we commend others, we do indeed honor, but we also bless and encourage them. In Paul's recognition of these two men, he did what he had previously taught the church in Thessalonica, "Encourage and build up one another."[2] **Let's look for ways to build others up. . .what do you say?**

Grace and Peace,
Christine

1 John 11.35
2 1 Thessalonians 5.11

From: Christine DiGiacomo <espressocd@cox.net>

Subject: Trust in Christ Alone.

Had prison made Paul crazy? I mean, maybe when Paul was stoned or flogged, he had been hit in the head one too many times . . .maybe he just was not thinking straight any longer, because he advised the Philippians, 'No matter what, >**My brothers and sisters, be full of joy in the Lord.** His admonition is to you and me too: Be full of joy in the Lord. Period. Hmmm . . .I can read some of your thoughts: "Be full of joy, Paul? How? Do you know how messed up my life has become? My family is in shambles, all I do is work to pay the bills, and I am still behind. I am so lonely . . .and you are saying, 'be full of joy'?"

Or from a Nigerian reader, "another extremist Muslim group—bent on establishing Sharia law in our country—has burned our churches with people inside; they destroyed banks and offices, and many were killed . . .and you say 'be full of joy in the Lord', Paul? How?"

Trust in the Lord Jesus Christ, Child . . .in Him alone. Your outward life may be in shambles, but your inner life of peace in Jesus can and must remain strong. Christian joy is indestructible.

Paul continues, >**It is no trouble for me to write the same things to you again, and it will help you to be more ready. Watch out for those who do evil, who are like dogs, who demand to cut the body.** Now when Paul warned about 'dogs', we must understand what he meant—in the middle east, stray dogs roamed the streets, hunted in garbage dumps, snarled and snapped at those they encountered along their way. Just so, there were those, (and clearly, Paul had strong feelings about them!), who taught that folks had to become Jews, and men had to be circumcised, which was a misrepresentation of the Good News of Jesus Christ. Their teaching was circumcision + Jesus = salvation, or the Law + Jesus = salvation. NO! Jesus + nothing, except our faith = salvation. **Trust in the Lord Jesus Christ, Child . . .in Him alone.**

Paul assured his Philippian brothers, >**We are the ones who are truly circumcised. We worship God through his Spirit, and our pride is in Christ Jesus. We do not put trust in**

ourselves or anything we can do. . .Trust in the Lord Jesus Christ, Child. . .in Him alone.

Our pride is in Christ Jesus. "You wanna go?" My older son says to the younger, after he has done something to provoke him . . .what he is saying is, 'do you really wanna get that started? (the 'dead leg' or ultimate flick in the head or snapping the wet towel on a bare leg, or any other physical thing that the bigger, stronger boy would surely best his little brother in. . .he turns around and says, 'you wanna go?') "Because if it is a physical contest you want, I will shut you down." (of course he will—three years older, 70 pounds heavier. . .) Similarly, Paul stacks up his pedigree—a big reason to boast—if trusting one's self is the path to take. >**although I might be able to put trust in myself. If anyone thinks he has a reason to trust in himself, he should know that I have greater reason for trusting in myself. I was circumcised eight days after my birth. I am from the people of Israel and the tribe of Benjamin. I am a Hebrew, and my parents were Hebrews. I had a strict view of the law, which is why I became a Pharisee. I was so enthusiastic I tried to hurt the church. No one could find fault with the way I obeyed the law of Moses.**

Those things were important to me—my Jewish heritage and upbringing—**but now I think they are worth nothing because of Christ. Not only those things, but I think that all things are worth nothing compared with the greatness of knowing Christ Jesus my Lord. Because of him, I have lost all those things, and now I know they are worthless trash. This allows me to have Christ and to belong to him. Now I am right with God, not because I followed the law, but because I believed in Christ. God uses my faith to make me right with him. Trust in the Lord Jesus Christ, Child . . .in him alone.**

I want to know Christ and the power that raised him from the dead. I want to share in his sufferings and become like him in his death. Then I have hope that I myself will be raised from the dead. Trust in the Lord Jesus Christ, Child . . .in him alone.

Now I am right with God . . .because I believed in Christ . . . yes, in him alone.

Grace and Peace,
Christine

From: Christine DiGiacomo <espressocd@cox.net>

Subject: What are you Aiming At??
Philippians 3.12-16

I am not an athlete. Oh, I am coordinated . . .a reasonable skier—water and snow—a strong skater, decent racquetball player, but that's about it. In small ways, I have lived vicariously through my four children's athletic pursuits and competitions, which have included baseball, basketball, soccer, volleyball, body-boarding, roller-hockey, and a brief foray into diving. I love watching football and baseball on television, and listen to a fair amount of sports talk on the radio, big fan of Jim Rome. With that said, I have often wished I could experience some of the moments great athletes experience—like stepping to the plate with a bat in my hands, only to see the outfielders back up, knowing I could crack a triple into deep left centerfield; or like running with every fiber of my being, aware of the footfalls on my heels, but pressing on to be the first to break the tape at the finish line; or collecting a soccer ball at my knees, controlling it enough to hook a hard shot with my right foot from 30 feet out, and sending it far-post into the net. Oh, those would be glorious moments!

Great as those moments would be, they pale in comparison to crossing the finish line of life, breaking the tape with my chest, and landing on the other side, among godly finishers from all eternity . . .yep, now that needs to be what I am 'aiming at'—or, as Paul said, I press on to reach the end of the race and receive the heavenly prize for which God, through Christ Jesus, is calling us.[1]

Ah, Paul . . .you know, God's ways are so brilliant. Think of how Jesus lived, loved and taught, and then left behind the charge to his disciples and followers to take the 'good news' into all the world . . .in short order, he sent the Holy Spirit, to equip them, and so that he could be ever-present with them . . .and then, God appointed Paul as the first missionary, who took the Gospel on the road.

Ah, Paul . . .So much of our understanding of the Christian path comes to us from Paul, who was personally confronted and then instructed by Jesus Christ. On his way to Damascus[2], Jesus got Paul's attention, and changed the trajectory of his life, from hater of those who followed Christ, to a follower of Christ himself

. . .yea, not just a follower, but a teacher of just what it means to be a Christian, and how to be victorious in the Christian life.

From Paul, we get 13 letters, or about a third of the New Testament. He gave us the "tions" to describe how God changes us: **salvation** – a *gift from God*, not attainable through the Law or even through good works on our part; **justification** – Jesus settles the balance sheet of our souls, making us right with God; and **sanctification** – the process the Holy Spirit works out in us as we stay close to him in this life; so that **transformation** is then indeed possible, as we morph from chrysalis to butterfly, spiritually speaking.

About his own walk with God, Paul tells us, "I don't mean to say that I have already achieved these things or that I have already reached perfection. But I press on to possess that perfection for which Christ Jesus first possessed me. No, dear brothers and sisters, I have not achieved it, but I focus on this one thing: Forgetting the past and looking forward to what lies ahead, I press on to reach the end of the race and receive the heavenly prize for which God, through Christ Jesus, is calling us.

Let all who are spiritually mature agree on these things. If you disagree on some point, I believe God will make it plain to you. But we must hold on to the progress we have already made. Philippians 3.12-16

I love that—forgetting the past and looking forward to what lies ahead, I press on . . .

Are you pressing on or is something holding you back? Are you dragging a 100-pound rucksack behind you, straining to make it, rather than living victoriously? >What is in your rucksack—guilt? Confess it, give it to God, leave it with him, and don't let your fear or sanctimonious pride permit you to pick that guilt back up again! >What is in your rucksack—words spoken over you or to you that have crippled you? In Jesus Christ, you are more than a conqueror![3] Cut the rucksack loose, and press on to what Jesus has for you. Press on . . .be faithful . . .stay at your post. Aim to break the tape at the finish line of your life, in full stride, with a strong gait, running into the arms of your Lord, who will say, "Well done." Yep, now that's a great thing to aim at.

Grace and Peace,
Christine

1 Philippians 3
2 Acts 9
3 Romans 8.37

From: Christine DiGiacomo <espressocd@cox.net>

Subject: Your life–a poem. Philippians 4.1
Your life – a poem. Philippians 4.1

"Therefore, my brothers, whom I love and long for, my joy and crown, stand firm thus in the Lord, my beloved." Paul's love for the Philippians just screams off the page, doesn't it? I can relate to Paul's feelings for those to whom he ministered . . .oh boy, can I! You see, ->when God calls an individual to serve, he places within his or her heart a supernatural love for the people to whom he sends her. Sometimes it means treading into deep water, murky water, but always it means an opportunity to point people to God.

Recently, I was asked to do a difficult thing, (referenced briefly in my writing two weeks ago). From across 3000 miles she asked, 'Would you be willing to give an agnostic blessing at my husband's memorial?' My mind instantly reeled. Agnostic blessing? Isn't that a contrast in terms? I knew what my answer had to be, and that God would supply what was needed. "Yes, I would be honored," I knew at once that it was a brilliant opportunity (and responsibility) to love well, in many respects. 'Hmmm . . .I am wondering if it might be okay to read a beautiful poem in Donald's memory—in tribute to his life'. . .to my relief, she agreed at once.

After stopping by the home of this family I have known—but not really known, because of their bent toward privacy—for 8 years, I noted that the front of the 'memory folder' described Donald as having lived with 'passion and purpose'. As I drove away, I thought to myself, 'Huh—passion and purpose—I often talk about those things, and how those who follow Jesus ought be people of both! But . . .here, the wife had chosen to describe her 46-year-old 'agnostic' husband the same way!' How much purpose is there really, in a life that ends with our last breath? How much purpose is there to our days if there is nothing that comes after them? How much passion can there be if we were not created on and for a purpose? 'Interesting how different, how shallow those words seem without God. And where do you turn when you are dying and have no relationship with the Eternal?

"Oh God, please, you must give me something for this family—that will honor Donald's memory, just as he was, and yet honors You! Lord, there are going to be so many people there from our small surf town and from the larger Southern California sports community—please God, give me something." So I googled 'poetry: passion and purpose' and in one response found that the oldest word for poetry in ancient Greek is poesis, which means "making." Now that rang a bell. I remembered the apostle Paul said, we are God's 'masterpiece' in Ephesians 2.10. Another Bible translation uses the word 'craftsmanship' . . .but that is only in English, because the word Paul used was also an ancient Greek word, poema. Hold that thought for a moment . . .poesis – making; poema – masterpiece. Ahhh. . .'see where I'm going?

I kept searching for something that would capture these things about Donald – husband, father, son, brother, competitor, friend, thoughtful, neighbor Don. . .No, twould be tough to find a poem to capture the full essence of this most remarkable individual. Indeed, no poem could capture Donald, for he was poesis – **he was the poem**, created.

[That concluded that portion of my eulogy. God had come through—beautiful inspiration for Donald's life, then I moved on and offered words of Christian hope to his 'spiritual' wife and children, and the standing-room only crowd of about 500. . .God gave me what was needful, and it was more than beautiful.]

Permit me to shift this to you now. . .friend, think of it— what words describe you? What adjectives? You can try to describe yourself, but only One can capture you, for only One fully knows you – the One that called you a masterpiece – a poema. _____, _____, _____, ___, _____, _____, _____, _____. Whatever <u>you</u> put in those blanks, as God's child, <u>he</u> sees you as beloved, cleansed, forgiven, delightful, remarkable, lovely, unique, and redeemed. Let no one take those from you, my beloved. Paul reminds us to stand firm in the Lord, *"For we are God's masterpiece. He has created us anew in Christ Jesus, so we can do the good things he planned for us long ago."* *Ephesians 2.10*

You are a beautiful masterpiece,
    created in the mind and image of God,
        now go and live accordingly, my dear ones.
            Let no one or no thing deter you. Amen.

Christine

From: Christine DiGiacomo <espressocd@cox.net>

Subject: Take a look at this—Philippians chapter four. Philippians 4.

Before we embark fully on this last beloved chapter of Paul's letter to the Philippians, looking at individual verses and groups of verses, please read it in full today. Before you read, please ask God to open your mind that you might understand his Word; ask him to open the eyes of your heart that you might apply it to your life. 'Your Word is light, your Word is life to me, O God!'

PHILIPPIANS 4. English Standard Version.

Therefore, my brothers, whom I love and long for, my joy and crown, stand firm thus in the Lord, my beloved.

I entreat Euodia and I entreat Syntyche to agree in the Lord. Yes, I ask you also, true companion, help these women, who have labored side by side with me in the gospel together with Clement and the rest of my fellow workers, whose names are in the book of life.

4) Rejoice in the Lord always; again I will say, Rejoice. Let your reasonableness be known to everyone. The Lord is at hand;

6) do not be anxious about anything, but in everything by prayer and supplication with thanksgiving let your requests be made known to God. And the peace of God, which surpasses all understanding, will guard your hearts and your minds in Christ Jesus.

8) Finally, brothers, whatever is true, whatever is honorable, whatever is just, whatever is pure, whatever is lovely, whatever is commendable, if there is any excellence, if there is anything worthy of praise, think about these things.

What you have learned and received and heard and seen in me—practice these things, and the God of peace will be with you. I rejoiced in the Lord greatly that now at length you have revived your concern for me. You were indeed concerned for me, but you had no opportunity. Not that I am speaking of being in need, for I have learned in whatever situation I am to be content.

I know how to be brought low, and I know how to abound. In any and every circumstance, I have learned the secret of facing plenty and hunger, abundance and need.

13 I can do all things through him who strengthens me.

Yet it was kind of you to share my trouble. And you Philippians yourselves know that in the beginning of the gospel, when I left Macedonia, no church entered into partnership with me in giving and receiving, except you only. Even in Thessalonica you sent me help for my needs once and again. Not that I seek the gift, but I seek the fruit that increases to your credit. I have received full payment, and more. I am well supplied, having received from Epaphroditus the gifts you sent, a fragrant offering, a sacrifice acceptable and pleasing to God.

19 And my God will supply every need of yours according to his riches in glory in Christ Jesus. To our God and Father be glory forever and ever. Amen.

21 Greet every saint in Christ Jesus. The brothers who are with me greet you. All the saints greet you, especially those of Caesar's household.

23 The grace of the Lord Jesus Christ be with your spirit.

Ah . . .the wonderful book of Philippians.
Tomorrow, we shall look more closely at the last chapter of this most beloved book.

Grace and Peace,
Christine

From: Christine DiGiacomo <espressocd@cox.net>

Subject: IN THE LORD. . .key words. Philippians 4.1-4

Daniel Szakalski was red-headed, skinny, freckle-faced and a bit of a rapscallion in class. Personally, I thought he was adorable, but I could tell by the way his mom cozied up to me on the first day of school, I just might have my hands full, having her fourth grade son in my class. It was many years ago now, but the reason I recall him so keenly, is because I remember when he found his love for reading and the lights came on . . .well, as his teacher, what a joy! In small part, that is what Paul is referencing when he calls his brothers 'his joy and crown'. From far away and in prison, with joy in his heart, and a gleam in his eye, he is proud of the young believers for 'sticking' with Christ, for standing IN THE LORD. "So then, my brothers, whom I love and yearn for, my joy and crown, so stand fast in the Lord, beloved." Philippians 4.1

Paul admonished them, 'stand fast in the Lord'. What's your story right now? Are you worried about pending medical results? Awaiting a callback from a would-be employer? 'Overwhelmed with worry about your teen-ager? Are you a new Christian convert in a Muslim country, wondering what will be your fate—joy in your own heart, yet already despised by your family? Picture with me Paul, composing these thoughts from his heart to yours—'Stand firm . . .let nothing throw you off course!' With love in my heart, with compassion in my chest, I say the same to you, 'Do not give up hope . . .nothing has caught God off guard. He sees you, he loves you.'

I closeted myself the other night, trying to be out of earshot from my family—where else? Yes, in my closet. I had only recently met this young man at the gym, but took an instant liking to him. . .yet I know he is in the battle of his lifetime. 'You have to memorize Scripture and change your thinking—right now,' I said into the phone. 'Don't you see, the thoughts you have—the thoughts you are letting run through your mind, have the chance to take you back to a place you do not want to go! The enemy will take you down, if you do not take your thoughts captive now,' I said to the young man, about 24, with a checkered past, beset by nightmares and treacherous thoughts by day.

What else could I give him? There is nothing greater than the strength of the Word of God. "Be strong and courageous. Do not be afraid; do not be discouraged, for the Lord your God is with you wherever you go." Joshua 1.9. Write it down, carry it with you, memorize it—or as Paul said, 'Stand firm thus in the Lord, my beloved.'

Our only port in the storm is to be in the Lord; our only hope in the face of temptation, to be in the Lord . . .

'And how about in times of disunity or times of discord? Even then, or is it especially then—we must be in the Lord. Remember, Paul called us (Christians/believers/followers of Christ, pick the one you like) to 'be like-minded, having the same love, being one in spirit and of one mind', back in chapter two of Philippians. Now take a look at specifics here: I plead with Euodia and I plead with Syntyche to be of the same mind in the Lord. Yes, and I ask you, my true companion, help these women since they have contended at my side in the cause of the gospel, along with Clement and the rest of my co-workers, whose names are in the book of life. In reality, in life, there will be differences . . .there will be differences of opinion; but in the Lord, we must reconcile. In order to reconcile and be reconciled, humility is required of us. . .true? Of course TRUE! Why would Paul 'call out' these two women whose names we are hard pressed to pronounce? Several reasons—they mattered, he loved them, he loved the body of believers, and he knew that discord could disrupt the work of the Lord.

While Paul pleads and urges Euodia and Syntyche to get along, to the Philippians as a whole, he gives a clear command: rejoice in the Lord. Rejoice in the Lord always. I will say it again: Rejoice! What does Paul mean by always, and how can he say such a thing? 'Always' means all the time, anywhere and everywhere, no matter the circumstances. He could command it of other believers because he demanded it of himself. Paul rejoiced in the Lord, by intention, regardless of his personal circumstances.

There is another side to this in the Lord thing—when we choose to be in the Lord, we are God's joy and crown; when we choose to be in the Lord, he makes all things right; when we live our lives in the Lord, we can and are able to rejoice in the Lord, no matter the circumstances. And that's the truth. I know.

Grace and Peace to you,
Christine

From: Christine DiGiacomo <espressocd@cox.net>

Subject: Joy! Joy! Joy!

Joy! Joy! Joy! Philippians 4.4

"Rejoice!" Paul said. He said it twice in one verse in fact. But that is not the whole story, for you see 'rejoice' is an action verb, the expression of our joy, our delight. So – chicken or egg? Which comes first? Do we rejoice, whether or not we feel our joy, in obedience that joy will come? Or do we find our joy and then obediently express it? (Yes, these are the questions that keep me awake at night!)

It is Christmas time, so we see the word 'joy' splashed about, we hear it in music, but do we feel it? Is it a feeling, or is it a 'knowing'?

One thing is for sure . . .people want joy.

People want to be around others who have it.

People want to know how to get it.

Let's talk about what we know of joy—

It's not about personality or temperament. I've heard folks say, 'Oh, it's easy for you to be joyful—it's just your personality. You're bubbly, and besides, you've got a great life!' Joy is not about personality.

Joy must be experienced in the moment; you can't save it up, it is not for tomorrow or next week. The psalmist said, "This is the day that the Lord has made. I will rejoice and be glad in it."[1]

Joy is not dependent on circumstances, which is why Paul could rejoice from prison! Happiness tends to depend more on external goings-on; circumstances are always changing, so happiness has the potential to elude us, sorta' like the bubble that we finally reach up to grab, only to find it popping in our hand. Joy seems to be inextricably tied to hope. Hope keeps joy alive; it feeds it. One current-day rabbi said, 'happiness as defined by our culture has become just a synonym for pleasure . . .' ah, sadly, that does seem true, doesn't it?

Happiness, at some point—sooner or later, is fleeting, while joy is lasting. I like what the ol' preacher, Charles Spurgeon, said on the difference between joy and happiness, "That word joyful is a very sweet and clear one. Happiness is a very dainty word, but yet it is somewhat insecure because it begins with a 'hap,' and seems to depend on a chance which <u>may</u> happen to the soul. We say 'happy-go-lucky', and that is very much the world's happiness. It is a kind of thing that may hap and may not hap. But there is no hap in joy. When we are joyful or full of joy, and that of the best kind, we are favored indeed. No man takes this joy from us . . .it is a celestial fruit, and earth cannot produce its like. (It is helpful to know that happiness is derived from the Latin word, 'hap'. Hap means hap-hazard . . .hmmm . . .)

Joy is linked with the heart of God—yea, it comes from the heart of God, because at the heart of God are all things good. For some, that is hard to swallow because religious or judgmental Christians have painted God as austere, far-off, possibly vindictive, or as a cosmic killjoy—when he is none of those.

When I was 12 years old, I played the organ at the evening service of a Pentecostal church. One of my favorite hymns had the chorus, 'it is joy unspeakable and full of glory, and the half has never yet been told.' The melody was pretty, and the words sung of a joy that is unequalled and can't really even be described—that kind of joy comes only from knowing the Lord.

Part of the joy of the Lord is how he feels about you, his beloved creature. The Father is ravished by you. You make him smile. You make him laugh. You make him leap for joy. You make his heart beat faster. The Bible even says, you make him sing for joy.[2] Whether or not you understand that does not stop God from feeling about you as he does. He loves your smile. The blemishes, wrinkles, and extra pounds you have may bother you, but he looks right past them. He loves you—just as you are. He loves you when you are awake, vibrant, and full of life, and he loves you when you're down, tired, and feeling lethargic. The truth is, God really likes you; in fact, he enjoys you. Thanks to the gracious act of his Son, he also sees you perfectly redeemed— when you accept his gift of salvation.

The great philosopher Blaise Pascal made this observation: "There once was in man a true happiness of which now remain to him only the mark and empty trace, which he in vain tries to fill from all his surroundings, seeking from things absent the help he does not obtain in things present. But these are all inadequate, because the infinite abyss can only be filled by an infinite and immutable object, that is to say only by God himself." There is no true happiness, there is no lasting joy without God's presence in our lives. Through walking with him in obedience, our joy will be made complete.

Walking closely to the Rabbi, you will know joy, and your rejoicing will be authentic . . .**Joy! Joy! Joy!**

Christine

1 Psalm 118.24
2 Zephaniah 3.17

From: Christine DiGiacomo <espressocd@cox.net>

Subject: Be gracious. . .now. Philippians 4.4-5

One of the most responded-to briefings I have written was on a subject that I bet never comes up in your daily conversations. I heard from folks near and far, moved by the need to embody the heart of the message. It took me a little while to find it since I sustained a hard-drive crash since writing it several years ago, but I located it on the Pastorwoman website, archived in the first book of the Bible I taught—James. [www.pastorwoman.com–loaded with free downloadable studies and podcasts to inform and encourage.]

Zoom out with me a moment, remembering where we are, and listen as Paul dictates from prison to a scribe, 'Rejoice in the Lord at all times. I will say it again – rejoice! Let your gracious gentleness be known to all men. The Lord is near.' (Philippians 4.4-5) The Greek word, epieikeia, is translated here as 'gracious gentleness', and is very difficult to translate into English. In other texts, we see 'graciousness, forbearance, softness, patience, gentleness . . .a different response than straight-line justice though justice is warranted.' I have been studying verse five all week, considering why Paul pairs these two great qualities of the Christian life together—he says 'rejoice' and in essence, 'be merciful to others'—'the Lord is coming back.' Simply—what is the significance of rejoicing and graciousness, and the Lord's return to us?

So that was your hint about the very popular briefing—did you catch it? Mercy. 'Entitled "Mercy Me—not just a band, but a great way to live," I wrote it back in the summer of 2008, though it seems to me that the world needs mercy now more than it needed it then! Why, the world around us is crying out for mercy . . .don't you sense it?

The common dictionary definition of mercy is 'compassion or forgiveness shown toward someone whom it is within one's power to punish or harm.' More often than not, the term mercy is used interchangeably with compassion, but alas it is more than that; when it would seem like one might expect judgment, the judge decides to pardon him, give him mercy. "Blessed are the merciful, for they will be shown mercy." Matthew 5.7 (part of the Beatitudes that Jesus gave us from the Sermon on the

Mount, found in Matthew and Luke) I want to be shown mercy . . .do you?

In order to give mercy, I believe one has to experience mercy. Paul had experienced God's mercy, so he could teach about it, and the need for it—calling it epieikeia, gracious gentleness. God wasn't initially so gentle with Paul, having to knock him to the ground on the road to Damascus in order to get his attention, close his mouth, and open his mind to the truth of Jesus Christ; but it was all to extend to him the tender mercy of eternal salvation. The same salvation message Paul took on the road and across the waters, establishing churches as he went, posing a threat to Rome, and landing himself in the prison from which he now wrote—and here he writes, 'Rejoice in the Lord, again I say, rejoice. Let your gracious gentleness be known to all men. The Lord is near.'

What is on Paul's mind? In the preceding couple verses, he told two women to work out their differences, as unity was imperative, disunity harmful to the church. He is well aware that he is probably going to be put to death for his supposed threat to Rome . . .STILL, in spite of any circumstances, the attitude of the believer must always be one of joy, evidenced in rejoicing.

And to joy, he adds, Christ-followers are to be gracious and gentle. They get along <u>inside</u> the church (a la the two women mentioned in verses two and three), and they love those <u>outside</u> the church. It is not a footnote or a subscript that Paul adds—'the Lord is near'; rather it is an admonition. 'Hey Christian, wake up—don't let your pettiness be the reason someone else wants nothing to do with Christianity; don't let your hate-speak drive people from the church. I am coming back . . .soon!'

Here is a timely example to illustrate my point: this fall, I have been active at San Clemente High School, establishing Fellowship of Christian Athletes, and another weekly worship experience, Sunday Night Live. There is a thirst for God, and it is so exciting. However, early on, a young Christian student from a church youth group that meets on campus, posted an anti-homosexual video on Facebook, filled with judgment, and little mercy; it was anything but helpful to the cause of Christ. Did the video message portray God's view of homosexuality accurately? Yes, but not his heart, nor his compassion, nor his way of building relationship to minister to those who are struggling. To use Paul's words—there was no gracious gentleness to be found.

The Lord is coming soon, friends—I believe that. We are to be light in the world. Light draws and attracts, it does not repel. Be joyful, Christian – let your joy be seen. Do not be the excuse someone needs to stay away from Jesus, rather be gracious, be merciful, Christian! Look for ways to embrace, to extend compassion, to include, to give away joy, joy, joy. . . . . . .

Christine

From: Christine DiGiacomo <espressocd@cox.net>

Subject: Mercy ~ Forgiveness. Philippians 4.5

Mercy ~ Forgiveness?? Let your gracious gentleness/ your mercy be evident to all! Philippians 4.5. Mercy . . .I keep thinking about it, with the sense that there is more to say, even now, even though Christmas is days away—maybe because Christmas is days away. James remarks in 2.13, " . . .judgment without mercy will be shown to anyone who has not been merciful. Mercy triumphs over judgment!"

The dictionary definition of mercy is 'compassion or forgiveness shown toward someone whom it is within one's power to punish or harm.' We have looked at mercy with regard to compassion, but I keep thinking about the forgiveness aspect of mercy. In general, I do not have too much trouble forgiving, except for things that have hurt me to the core—maybe only one or two—and I have a hard time letting go of those things.

But forgiveness is part of mercy . . .Forgiveness is immense. It breaks down walls, frees hearts, mends countries, restores families, and draws out the best in us. It can turn hatred into tenderness and the desire to destroy into a passion to protect. It is more powerful than any weapon, government, or wealth. Nothing else can bring such profound healing. Forgiveness forms the foundation of our relationship with God and sustains our relationships with each other. When we unleash this gift, by receiving it in humble trust that God can actually free our heart and heal our relationships, then the miraculous can happen.[1]

Forgiveness is vertical–whether it is seeking forgiveness for our own sins. . .or endeavoring to forgive another for what we have ought against them. . .we go to God first. 'Forgiveness is God's invention for coming to terms with a world in which people are unfair to each other and hurt each other deeply. He began by forgiving us. And he invites us all to forgive each other.'[2]

Forgive–pardon; excuse for a fault or offense; renounce anger or resentment against; absolve from payment for a debt.

Who do **you** need to forgive? _____

What did he/she do? _____

Consider what Jesus had to say: "For if you forgive men when they sin against you, your heavenly Father will also forgive you. But if you do not forgive men their sins, your Father will not forgive your sins." Matthew 6.14-15 Paul said, "Bear with each other and forgive whatever grievances you may have against one another. Forgive as the Lord forgave you." Colossians 3.13

Still not convinced you should forgive? You might wish to look at this 2007 Los Angeles Times article called "Forgive and Be Well". . .it cites research that forgiveness can improve cardiovascular function, diminish chronic pain, relieve depression and boost quality of life. . .while failure to forgive may, over a lifetime, boost a person's risk for heart disease, mental illness and other ills. . .Forgiveness is a skill that can be learned. Hmmm . . .[3]

So **you** realize you need to forgive someone, but how do you do it? Are there any steps to be taken? I think there are—1. Recognize that you need to forgive the person who injured you (whether or not they know it—whether or not he seeks forgiveness) 2. Commit to forgiveness. Come on, make a commitment to forgive him. Don't just decide . . .commit. 3. Ask God to help you forgive, to release the bitter or hurt feeling you have, and give it to him. Pray for the person, for his wellbeing; commit him/her to God, and let it go.

One of my favorite teachers is Dr. James MacDonald, and he talked about one tool he has used to forgive people who have hurt him: "I wrote down the names of six particular people. I remember very clearly getting on my knees and envisioning a little leather pouch and, after writing out the people's names on little pieces of paper, I put them in the bag and tightened it up. I wrote the word Forgiveness on the outside. In my mind's eye, I knelt down and laid that bag at the cross, saying, "God, in view of all that you've forgiven me, I'm letting this go. I'm leaving it behind. I'm releasing them from the obligation that resulted when they injured me."

Forgiveness is powerful . . .don't you see? Choosing unforgiveness is paralyzing. Make the right choice—right now.

Practice grace and you will know peace, Christine

1 – <u>TrueFaced</u> – Thrall, McNichol, Lynch

2–Lewis B. Smedes

3–http://articles.latimes.com/2007/dec/31/health/he-forgiveness31

From: Christine DiGiacomo <espressocd@cox.net>

Subject: "With thanksgiving"–what difference does it make? Philippians 4.6-7

It is early Saturday morning as I write, two weeks before Christmas. I have been up for hours, though the rest of my household slumbers—even my dogs, Graycie and Missie. Once my mind awakened, there was no more sleep to be had, as I went back to pondering the same thing as when I went to sleep—<u>why did Paul throw in the words, 'with thanksgiving'</u>? Let me explain.

I first memorized these verses from the King James Version, no doubt from the Bible my mother gave me when I was five—"Be careful for nothing; but in every thing by prayer and supplication <u>with thanksgiving</u> let your requests be made known unto God. And the peace of God, which passeth all understanding, shall keep your hearts and minds through Christ Jesus." Philippians 4.6-7 In high school, I loved <u>The Way</u>, (any of you remember that—with the faces inside the lettering of the paperback Living Bible?), and memorized "Don't worry about anything; instead, pray about everything; tell God your needs and don't forget to thank him for his answers. If you do this you will experience God's peace, which is far more wonderful than the human mind can understand. His peace will keep your thoughts and your hearts quiet and at rest as you trust in Christ Jesus." **The verses were inspirational for me.**

Toward the end of my high school years, the New American Standard came out, and then I memorized, "Be anxious for nothing, but in everything by prayer and supplication with thanksgiving let your requests be made known to God. And the peace of God, which surpasses all comprehension, will guard your hearts and your minds in Christ Jesus."

Whichever the version, **the words were comforting and instructive to me**.

However, **the words became life to me** when I claimed them for my blonde curly-haired little girl of seven, Amy, who asked me the meaning of life, as I said her evening prayers with her one night. 'Ah Lord,' I prayed as I put my own head down on the pillow, 'what can I give her little troubled mind, so old for one so young?' And he gave me these verses to pray for her, over her, and with her. They became the verses I prayed for Amy as she went through grammar school, high school, away to U.C. Berkeley . .

."Do not be anxious about anything, but in everything, by prayer and petition, <u>with thanksgiving</u>, present your requests to God. And the peace of God, which transcends all understanding, will guard your hearts and your minds in Christ Jesus." (NIV)

Paul's intent is clear–Christian, worry is not for you. In fact, it is wrong for you to worry. God has given you the gift of prayer, of communicating with him. Go to him with everything that concerns you in your life—tell him your needs, ask him for his intervention, with thanksgiving, and he will give you a peace that defies all human logic. But, why thanksgiving? All these years—from all of these different versions—I have just spouted it off as a 'given', but never stopped to consider why the 'thanks' part was important to either the prayer, the answer, God, or me either, for that matter . . .until now.

These days, when I give these verses away, I most commonly quote the New Living Translation, "Don't worry about anything; instead, pray about everything. Tell God what you need, and thank him for all he has done. Then you will experience God's peace, which exceeds anything we can understand. His peace will guard your hearts and minds as you live in Christ Jesus."

Though I like this translation a lot, it misses the full measure of "with thanksgiving" that I believe Paul had in mind, as he wrote verse six. First, children of God must **always be thankful for the gift of prayer**, the gift of communicating with our loving Heavenly Father; and second, we must bear in mind that **whatever his responses to our prayers, we ought be giving him 'thanks'**, because 'he works all things together for good to those who love him[1]!' He who watches over Israel neither slumbers nor sleeps[2]; he who watches you and me has not gone to sleep on the job either. So, before worry, let us pray . . .and then before any known outcome, let us give thanks to the God above who is all-wise and all-knowing and has our best interests in mind.

Now I get it. . .now I see the importance of coupling prayer and thanksgiving—they form a powerful 'one-two punch' for victorious daily living, understanding God's loving care for us, enabling us to be at peace.

Christine

1–Romans 8.28
2 – Psalm 121.4

From: Christine DiGiacomo <espressocd@cox.net>

Subject: God–the great gift-giver. Philippians 4.6-7

'Do not be anxious about anything, but in everything, by prayer and petition, <u>with thanksgiving</u>, present your requests to God. And the peace of God, which transcends all understanding, will guard your hearts and your minds in Christ Jesus.' I cannot read the verses without thinking, 'What a gift!' What these verses offer us is nothing short of a beautiful gift, intended to give us peace in our minds, and peace in our hearts, if we practice them.

The other day I was driving along the Pacific Coast Highway, looking at the crashing waves and thinking about the treasure of Philippians 4.6-7, (the above verses). But then I thought, 'There are so many good gifts God gives to us'. . .mindful that I was looking at the grandeur of his created beauty at the time—with the sun, wind, clouds and water seeming to whip up a master-piece just for my viewing pleasure. Ah, the gift of God's creation.

At the last Sunday Night Live, I showed the high school students "How Great is our God," an incredible DVD about the magnificence and sheer size of the created universe, making the viewer aware of just how truly awesome is our God. The stars, the galaxies are massive and he spoke them into exis-tence! Wow. And then there's God's grandest creation—us. To see, to be reminded of the miracle of life, and how 'he knit us together in our mother's womb', even from the first moment of conception is so grounding. Oh yes, God's gifts of <u>creation</u> are wonderful indeed.

But wait, there's more! Daily, I am thankful for the gift of his <u>Word</u>, and that we live at a point in time that we have the printed Scripture. It is the sweet <u>Holy Spirit</u> that revisits a Scripture to my mind, just when I need it—a beautiful gift as well. Love for one another is a gift straight from the heart of a loving God. I am keenly aware that it is the <u>love of fellow Christians</u> that oft sustains me; life is not meant to be lived solo. Jesus lived in community with his disciples—his main men and best friends—as he loved them and taught them. <u>Community</u> is definitely one of the gifts God has given me, and I cherish it.

But wait, there's more! <u>Being able to serve God is a gift</u>, and a most humbling one, for me. I think of my flaws, I think of sins committed, and I think, 'even still, in his mercy, he uses me,' and I marvel at that. Almost daily, I smile to myself when I think about how strange it is that I have favor with so many of these high school students—what in the world?! But you know what? Sometimes it is my flaws God uses. Mistakes that I have learned from, sins I have committed that keep me from judging others, trials I have endured that I would wish on no one . . .all of these, God redeems and God uses. I think of Moses who told God he wasn't really qualified to lead—God said, 'What's in your hand, Moses?' For whatever is in our hand, Friend, that is what God uses—oh, and what is in our heart. Yes, serving God is a gift.

But wait, there's more! The things that God produces within the heart and life of the child who walks closely with him . . .those things are GIFTS. Those gifts include the <u>fruit</u> of the Spirit— love, joy, peace, patience, kindness, goodness, faithfulness, gentleness, and self control. Have you ever just had a feeling of joy come over you—almost to the point of feeling giddy? 'Can't explain it? Have you been in the midst of the trial or in an ordinarily stressful situation, but you had peace of mind? Friends, that is what we call 'peace that passes understanding'—peace that defies logic, and it is a gift!

There is also the <u>fruit</u> that the Christian produces by 'abiding in the Vine'—Jesus Christ, by choosing to follow closely in the steps of the Rabbi. Some Bible translations refer to this fruit also as good works. It is not necessarily that you and I should count these, (probably not), but it seems we ought be aware of whether or not we are growing and maturing, ceasing to make the same old mistakes, or being over-comers . . .do you follow me?

Indeed, from the heart of a loving Heavenly Father, endless gifts abound . . .'Behold, what manner of love the Father has given unto them!'

Grace and Peace to you,
Christine

From: Christine DiGiacomo <espressocd@cox.net>

Subject: Mind the Storehouse of your Mind.
Philippians 4.8

Paul was just published in the ladies' magazine, Good Housekeeping, did you see it? In a section about prayers to refresh your life, Paul made the cut with Philippians 4.8. 'Funny thing is, I had never thought of the verse as a prayer, but rather as a benchmark for excellence in our thinking.

"Finally, brothers, whatever is true, whatever is noble, whatever is right, whatever is pure, whatever is lovely, whatever is admirable—if anything is excellent or praiseworthy—think about such things."

The 'finally, brothers', is because Paul is winding down his letter to his Christian brothers in Philippi, remember? He has just told them in the preceding verses not to worry, but to pray—to take everything to God in prayer, and then God will give the blessing of peace that cannot be experienced by unbelievers . . .a peace that defies logic. And now Paul tells them to mind the storehouses of their thought lives.

Our minds set themselves on something, have you noticed? So we are wise to consider that to which our minds are given. To what does your mind drift? We are to govern our thoughts. This anonymous little piece is a great reminder for me: "Sow a thought, and you reap an act; sow an act, and you reap a habit; sow a habit, and you reap a character; sow a character, and you reap a destiny." So. . .it seems that character is formed by making choices in one direction—thinking rightly again and again.

To be a good thinker requires a couple things: first desire and then discipline. Good thinking does not just happen. Good thinking happens by intention. It happens by exposing ourselves to good, right and true thinking . . .or what did Paul say? 'Think about whatever is true, noble, right, pure, lovely, or admirable'—those things which have their source in the Creator. Become a student of that which is lovely and noble, that which is pure and excellent—enjoy, delight, learn and share those things with others.

I had a birthday last week, and my dear friend gave me the new biography <u>Bonhoeffer: pastor, martyr, prophet, spy</u>[1] because she knows me well. Though it is 544 pages long, I am going to be sad when it is finished because it is so rich with the beauty of artistic, academic and theological learning and writing—that were part of this remarkable young man's life (Dietrich Bonhoeffer) in WWII Germany . . .good books are a great way to think new, rich thoughts! (I am just 95 pages in thus far)

Endeavoring to think God's thoughts after him is perhaps the highest form of thinking to which man might aspire. Meditate on just what that might mean.

Sifting our thoughts, as to whether or not they are pleasing to God, is a most worthy endeavor indeed. 'Search me, O God, and know my thoughts,' the Psalmist said, in Psalm 139. And 'May the words of my mouth and the meditation of my heart [thoughts] be acceptable in your sight, O Lord, my Rock and my Redeemer.[2]'

Friends, you and I are the gatekeepers of our thoughts, which is why we must exercise great wisdom about what we let into our minds in the first place, taking care about what we read, listen to, watch or whatever . . .When I was a very little girl, I used to sing the song at Sunday school, "O be careful little eyes what you see . . .' and then, 'little ears what you hear. . . for the Father up above is looking down with love, so be careful little eyes what you see. . .' There are times when we need to say, "Enough! I am not watching that anymore! I am not reading that author any more; her writing fills me with negativity, or that kind of music takes me places my mind should not go . . ."

Paul had it right–whatever is true, noble, right, pure, lovely, or admirable—let's fix our thoughts on those things.

Grace and Peace,
Christine

1 – <u>Bonhoeffer: Pastor, Martyr, Prophet, Spy</u> by Eric Metaxas
2 – Psalm 19.14

From: Christine DiGiacomo <espressocd@cox.net>

Subject: Is He FOR REAL? Philippians 4.9-13

Pressing on. . .Paul writes,
"Whatever you have learned or received or heard from me, or seen in me—put it into practice." *So, in total, Paul is saying—Do the things I have told you to do, including 'Rejoice in the Lord . . .always! Do not be anxious about anything; but pray about everything that concerns you. Fix your thoughts on those things which are pleasing to God—those things which are true, noble, pure, lovely, admirable . . .'* **And the God of peace will be with you**. *See, our part is to pray, with thanksgiving, and choose to think right thoughts; God's part is to supply our peace. That is very straightforward. Paul continues,* 'I rejoice greatly in the Lord that at last you have renewed your concern for me. Indeed, you have been concerned, but you had no opportunity to show it. I am not saying this because I am in need . . .**for I have learned to be content whatever the circumstances. I know what it is to be in need, and I know what it is to have plenty. I have learned the secret of being content in any and every situation, whether well fed or hungry, whether living in plenty or in want.**

The dictionary defines contentment as 'satisfaction'. But the Greek word used to describe contentment in the Bible doesn't just mean to be satisfied, or to have sufficient, but to have an ATTITUDE that lets us be satisfied with whatever is available. I remember being deeply impressed with Paul's disposition, and his ability to be content, even when he was shackled, in pain, and in prison: " . . .I have learned to be content whatever the circumstances. I know what it is to be in need, and I know what it is to have plenty. I have learned the secret of being content in any and every situation, whether well fed or hungry, whether living in plenty or in want."

Paul passionately pursued God, and lived on purpose; his priorities kept him focused. Even when he was physically and mentally tortured, he knew, 'My God will supply all my needs, according to his riches in Christ Jesus.'* Paul knew the source of all good things, and trusted him. Indeed, he firmly believed and lived, **"I can do everything through him who gives me strength."** 4.13

Contentment is for the 'now'—You see, it is not uncommon for us to think, 'I'll be happy when . . .' 'Everything will be better when . . .' 'If only . . . ' 'If I could get this . . .' 'or be . . .' THEN I'd be happy. Not so. Contentment is not found in possessions, accomplishments, or station in life. Those are 'icing on the cake', but certainly not the pathway to inner joy. Experiencing contentment usually involves the elevation of our thinking, evaluating our life purpose, (a passionate pursuit of God), and establishing accompanying priorities. **Contentment may be yours~ do you want it?**

Grace and Peace,
Christine

*Philippians 4.19

From: Christine DiGiacomo <espressocd@cox.net>

Subject: WhatEver. Philippians 4.11-12

If you have a teenager, or if you have been around very many of them recently, you are familiar with the 'whatEver' used as a sarcastic retort to something you said that they didn't like. But yesterday the word "whatever" struck me quite differently, twice.

Early in the morning, I was studying Paul's words, "I am not saying this because I am in need, for I have learned to be content whatever the circumstances. I know what it is to be in need, and I know what it is to have plenty. I have learned the secret of being content in any and every situation, whether well fed or hungry, whether living in plenty or in want." Did you see it—the 'whatever'? I began to wax long about the 'whatever' in our various circumstances; looking at the passage, Paul seems to be indicating outward circumstances. No matter if he was hungry or full, he was able to be content.

I prayed with my pen in response, "He was a man, Lord—did he not FEEL all the angst a woman feels—that I feel—in the very throes of life? And Lord, did Paul have a mind that gets so divided, so pulled this way and that like mine often does, until I am exhausted by my own thoughts—such that it would be difficult to say at that time that I am content?" See, I am only recently coming to terms with the realization that my mind really does never rest. . .and well, maybe that is not so normal. (whatever normal is)

But as I prayed and thought, I believe Paul was very much talking about the inward part of the 'WHATEVER'. Yes, Paul had learned, 'whatever the circumstances –even when enduring inward or outward pain- to be content.' And of course, he had an over-active, always moving mind! He did not just live his life full-tilt for the cause of Christ, no matter what it cost him—he wrote about his life and circumstances, he fully developed Christian doctrine, established churches, taught them, and encouraged them to flourish.

Allow me to cut to this last Sunday Night Live leaders' meeting . . .I had asked Dave to lead a discussion with the students, prompting them to think about their spiritual goals for 2012. 'Well,' he said, as he began—kinda' looked down, smiled, and shook his close-cropped head. (Dave is a burly, football guy with a big old heart. I met him at the gym one day—sitting abreast of him and another big, gnarly young guy—three of us in a row, on stationary bikes, studying our Bibles. I turned and said, 'All right, what's going on here?' noting their reading material, as unusual as mine, for the gym. I soon learned that Big Dave had recently started a Fellowship of Christian Athletes Bible study at our nearby community college, and really loved God. Forty-five minutes later, the three of us were buddies, standing in the middle of the large facility, saying a prayer. I invited them to S.N.L., the high school group I lead, and well, more on that later . . .back to Dave for now—)

'Well, when we met Christine,' Big Dave said, 'One of the things she mentioned about us sharing with you guys, was that it was best to keep it 'real, raw, and relevant'. And then, he told them that he felt God had led him to end a five-plus year dating relationship because he had let it come between him and God. I thought Big Dave was going to cry, but he didn't, though his pain was palpable. He explained that for 2012, his goal is absolutely to keep God Number One; it made quite an impression.

And then, I thought about the 'whatever' again. For my young friend, Dave, he wasn't experiencing Paul's outward turmoil of shipwreck or torture or imprisonment, but he was definitely experiencing heartache. Could he then say, 'whatever—yes, even now—I am content in my Lord'? For that is his challenge at present.

WhatEver . . .may we find our contentment in our Lord Jesus Christ.

Grace and Peace,
Christine

From: Christine DiGiacomo <espressocd@cox.net>

Subject: Generosity from the Philippians–**this is a good one—keep reading to second page!

As Paul wraps his letter to his fellow Christians in Philippi, he commends them for their generosity toward him—take a look:

"I rejoice greatly in the Lord that at last you have renewed your concern for me. Indeed, you have been concerned, but you had no opportunity to show it. I am not saying this because I am in need, for I have learned to be content whatever the circumstances . . .Yet it was good of you to share in my troubles. Moreover, as you Philippians know, in the early days of your acquaintance with the gospel, when I set out from Macedonia, not one church shared with me in the matter of giving and receiving, except you only; for even when I was in Thessalonica, you sent me aid again and again when I was in need. Not that I am looking for a gift, but I am looking for what may be credited to your account. I have received full payment and even more; I am amply supplied, now that I have received from Epaphroditus the gifts you sent. They are a fragrant offering, an acceptable sacrifice, pleasing to God. **And my God will meet all your needs according to his glorious riches in Christ Jesus**. To our God and Father be glory for ever and ever. Amen."

I wonder if the Philippians had access to Paul's writing to the church at Corinth—did they know what he had taught about sowing and reaping generously? Is that why they had given so generously to Paul, and taken care of him? Or did it just feel right to them, to take care of the one who had brought them the Gospel of Jesus Christ? From 2 Corinthians chapter 9—

Remember this: Whoever sows sparingly will also reap sparingly, and whoever sows generously will also reap generously.

Each man should give what he has decided in his heart to give, not reluctantly or under compulsion, for **God loves a cheerful giver.**

And God is able to make all grace abound to you, so that in all things at all times, having all that you need, you will abound in every good work. As it is written: "He has scattered abroad his gifts to the poor; his righteousness endures forever." Now he who supplies seed to the sower and bread for food will also supply and increase your store of seed and will enlarge the harvest of your righteousness. You will be made rich in every way so that you can be generous on every occasion, and through us your generosity will result in thanksgiving to God."

I do not write too much about money—how people spend and whether or not they give to God, unless the Scripture passage warrants it, and the finishing out of Paul's letter to the Philippians certainly does. His commendation of the Philippians' financial consideration of him as their pastor, their shepherd and teacher, has broader application than for just the first century believer.

I am not a religious person; if I were, then I would tell you what my religion requires as the proper amount or percentage that I should give of my income. I am, however, a God follower, and a Bible believer and teacher. Accordingly, in short, here is MY disposition toward giving to God, and also what I tell those who ask me, which is more frequent than you might guess.

It is my understanding that the Old Testament mandated a ten percent tithe from the first fruits of what was earned. There is no such percentage given in the New Testament. I believe in the principle of Luke 12.48—that 'to whom much is given, much will be required'. I have been given much. I do not believe that 'much' is confined to financial resources, however; I believer 'much' refers also to our time, our talent, and yes, our treasure. Ken Blanchard and Truett Cathy added 'touch' to that—which is brilliant![1]

I believe there is great reward for those who give to the work of the Lord faithfully. In Galatians 6, Paul teaches that we should support those who teach us the Word of God. My friends, God rewards obedience by meeting our financial needs. The amount given is not the important part, but faithfulness and generosity of heart are both crucial. Honestly, where would this (non-profit) ministry be without its several supporters? "Thank you so kindly" to those who give; I am so very grateful. Your giving is what supports the 'Google Ads' that attracts global readers to the PastorWoman website and adds them to this distribution, free of charge, of course. Your (tax-deductible) giving is what supports the website that spreads the Gospel in this information-driven era in which we live. Only in this day and age could the gospel spread in such a manner—isn't it remarkable?[2]

But here's the thing—when we realize . . .when we remember that all good gifts are from the Father, our gratitude to him compels us to want to give, to love, to touch, to bless, does it not? I believe it was gratitude to Paul and to God that moved the Philippians to action; I believe it was their love for God, and their love for Paul that compelled them to make sure his needs were met, to make sure that the Gospel continued to go forward through Paul. Our gratitude must cause our hearts to swell with generosity as well, my dear ones~

Grace and Peace to you,
Christine

1–The Generosity Factor – Ken Blanchard and S. Truett Cathy

2–Should you wish to contribute to PastorWoman ministries, you can do so through the website: www.pastorwoman.com, or by mailing your tax-deductible check to PastorWoman Corp., P.O. Box 1195, San Clemente, CA, 92674.

From: Christine DiGiacomo <espressocd@cox.net>

Subject: The Lost Art of Letter Writing.
Philippians 4.21-23

Nobody mourned its impending death. . .no one talked about how much it would be missed. No billboards or television commercials warned of the void it would leave . . .yet, just like that, it has almost vanished as a viable connection of hearts, of happenings and goings-on, as exchange of cordialities, and recording of historical events—it is the irreplaceable hand-written letter.

I am a tactile person. I love pen and paper—especially good quality paper and a pen that writes smoothly upon that paper. I do not profess to do too many things well, but in case you are wondering—I have strong abdominal muscles. I have pretty penmanship, and I am a great speller. I have strong abdominal muscles and can do more sit-ups than the average mammal. And . . .I used to be able to write a great letter; I am not sure anymore.

Paul wrote a great letter, conforming to the Greco-Roman letter writing conventions, beginning and ending with his greetings:

"Greet all the saints in Christ Jesus. The brothers who are with me send greetings. All the saints send you greetings, especially those who belong to Caesar's household. The grace of the Lord Jesus Christ be with your spirit. Amen."

Paul endeavors to connects several things in these last few verses: the saints, those who are 'in Christ Jesus'; Paul's fellow ministers who send greetings to the Philippian Christians, and the other believers—such as those who belong to Caesar's household—which could mean members serving Caesar all over the world. Take note: as early as it was—in terms of the spread of Christianity—Christianity had spread into the very center of the Roman government, or as Paul said, to 'those who belong to Caesar's household'.

It would be 300 more years before Constantine 'legalized' Christianity in Rome, but Christianity's early in-roads were undeniable. Because Paul had been literally chained to the Roman guard(s), they had heard the Gospel—there had been no escaping for them—and it had spread far and wide through the Roman Empire. And now, these 'members of Caesar's household' were sending greetings to their fellow Christians in Philippi—can you spell i-r-o-n-i-c or rather d-i-v-i-n-e? 'The grace of the Lord Jesus Christ be with your spirit. Amen.'

F. B. Meyer, turn of the century English minister, commented far better than I ever could myself: "It is impossible to define all that is meant by this comprehensive prayer—illumination for the soul, love for the heart, strength for the mind, purity for the character, help in every time of need, direction in all perplexity and difficulty—all these are included in the word grace." These are the things that Paul breathed out in prayer for his beloved Philippians . . .knowing he could not be with them, as they no doubt endured persecution for their beliefs, hardships, trials . . .things unspeakable which would require the grace of the Lord Jesus.

Have you ever loved someone into faith? Oh sure you prayed, and then what? In order to see them across the finish line, I think you would have had to truly love them, been devoted to them in some part of yourself, been committed to pray for them— well, have you? Then, you would 'get' Meyer's understanding of grace—'illumination for the soul, love for the heart, strength for the mind, purity for the character, help in every time of need, direction in all perplexity and difficulty'.

For that is what we wish for those we love, for those we want to see cross the finish line of faith. Is it not?

And for you, my dear friends . . .For you, my beloved readers around the world . . .

I wish nothing less—Illumination for your soul, love for your heart and in your heart, strength for your mind, purity in your character, help in your time of need, direction in all perplexity and in any difficulty you might face . . .grace and forgiveness to cover any frailty in your being. Amen. So be it. In the name of Jesus.

Grace and Peace,
Christine

From: Christine DiGiacomo <espressocd@cox.net>

Subject: A 'Wrap' on Philippians.

'Seems like only yesterday we began studying Paul's letter to the Philippians, though now 'it is finished'. . .we have come to the end. What a letter it has been! I feel like I learned more about Paul's softer side, as he expressed his love for his Philippian brothers and sisters repeatedly and in several different ways. Everything Paul lived for revolved around Jesus Christ.

Though just four chapters, and written while Paul was incarcerated by the Roman government, Philippians is chalk-full of verses that are hopeful, forward-looking, inspirational, devotional, and purposeful. Let's take another look together at several of them, shall we?

Being confident of this, that he who began a good work in you will carry it on to completion until the day of Christ Jesus. 1.6

For to me, to live is Christ and to die is gain 1.21

Do nothing out of selfish ambition or vain conceit, but in humility consider others better than yourselves. Each of you should look not only to your own interests, but also to the interests of others. 2.3-4

Your attitude should be the same as that of Christ Jesus: he humbled himself and became obedient to death—even death on a cross! 2.5,8

Continue to work out your salvation with fear and trembling, for it is God who works in you to will and to act according to his good purpose. 2.12-13

One thing I do: Forgetting what is behind and straining toward what is ahead, I press on toward the goal to win the prize for which God has called me heavenward in Christ Jesus. 3.13-14

Our citizenship is in heaven. And we eagerly await a Savior from there, the Lord Jesus Christ. . .3.20

Rejoice in the Lord always. I will say it again: Rejoice! 4.4

Do not be anxious about anything, but in everything, by prayer and petition, with thanksgiving, present your requests to God. And the peace of God, which transcends all understanding, will guard your hearts and your minds in Christ Jesus. 4.6-7

Finally, brothers, whatever is true, whatever is noble, whatever is right, whatever is pure, whatever is excellent or praiseworthy—think about such things. 4.8

I have learned to be content whatever the circumstances. I know what it is to be in need, and I know what it is to have plenty. I have learned the secret of being content in any and every situation, whether well fed or hungry, whether living in plenty or in want. 4.11-12

I can do everything through him who gives me strength. 4.13

And my God will meet all your needs according to his glorious riches in Christ Jesus. 4.19

Perhaps you have other verses from this letter of Paul's that spoke to you, but these few I truly treasure, and have memorized most of them. You just gotta love Paul, don't you?

Grace and Peace,
Christine

From: Christine DiGiacomo, espressocd@cox.net

Subject: Welcome to Colossians. Colossians 1.1-2

Greetings, Dear Ones.

Paul's writings, which account for more than thirty percent of the New Testament, are invaluable to all who want to know and grow in their Christian faith. Though Paul wrote to new believers in Jesus Christ almost two thousand years ago, his teachings inform us about what it means to live for Christ today . . .about the difference between life under the Law and the free gift of God's grace. Paul teaches of getting along with others, (in and out of the church), being an effective witness, loving without hypocrisy, matters of the Holy Spirit, and keeping Jesus Christ as our focus . . .What's more, Paul's life is proof that God can change anyone, as Jesus' interruption of Paul's travel to Damascus literally caused the Christ-hater to do a 180-degree turn and become Christ's biggest promoter and Christianity's first and most important missionary.

I invite you to locate the little book of Colossians in your Bible and read completely through it—won't take you long, as it is just four chapters. As when he wrote Philippians, Paul writes from prison, having gotten word about things happening among the believers in the little town of Colossae, [from] "Paul, an apostle of Christ Jesus by the will of God, and Timothy our brother, to God's holy people in Colossae, the faithful brothers and sisters in Christ:

Grace and peace to you from God our Father." verses 1 and 2

His was a standard greeting in the ancient world, almost like presenting a business card at the start of a business lunch—introducing himself and greeting those to whom he was writing. His title – "apostle of Christ Jesus by the will of God" – whoa, a strong, affirmative statement, by one who had been challenged on that point. His position was strong, and it was right, because he had been called to it, through a face-to-face encounter with the risen Lord, though true enough, he had not been one of Jesus' 12 disciples. He couples himself with Timothy, his dear Christian brother—perhaps because his readers knew Timothy, or Timothy was the scribe for Paul's words, or simply the one who delivered the letter to the Colossians.

His greeting commends their Christian faithfulness, and extends the best he has to offer them—"***grace and peace from God our Father***". Paul really had a thing about **grace.** I guess because **grace** had turned his world upside down! Yes, grace had changed everything for Paul, and so he leads with it. I have written about *grace dancing* – and that reminds me that grace draws me to itself, it invites my participation. "I know nothing, except what everyone knows—if there when *Grace* dances, I should dance," wrote the poet W. H. Auden.

God doesn't wait for me to come to him . . .he runs to me, with arms outstretched. And in his arms, I remember how to dance again. Now that, dear friend, is amazing grace.

From: Christine DiGiacomo, espressocd@cox.net

Subject: Big Dave. . .faith, love, hope.
Colossians 1.3-8

A prayer to start: Lord God, as we read your word this day, open our eyes to see what you would have us see, and apply it to our lives, just as the Colossians did when Paul's letter was read to them. Amen

Paul writes, in about the year 62 A.D.~

"We always thank God, the Father of our Lord Jesus Christ, when we pray for you, because we have heard of your faith in Christ Jesus and of the love you have for all God's people—the faith and love that spring from the hope stored up for you in heaven and about which you have already heard in the true message of the gospel that has come to you. In the same way, the gospel is bearing fruit and growing throughout the whole world—just as it has been doing among you since the day you heard it and truly understood God's grace. You learned it from Epaphras*, our dear fellow servant, who is a faithful minister of Christ on our behalf, and who also told us of your love in the Spirit."

I would like to suggest that you print out this passage, circle the words that stand out to you, and ask God to reproduce its tenets in your life.

Here's what I see: Paul says they thank God for the faithfulness of the Colossian believers, which of course, means that he was praying for them! 'Love that. (May I ask, for whom are you praying—that they will stay strong in their faith—that they will grow in the knowledge of the things of our God? Hmmm? Friends, we must pray fervently for our young people and our loved ones, that they might stand up against the temptations and tough situations they face, that they might 'stay at their post', come what may.)

There are three things that Paul notes about their lives: *faith, love* and *hope*. While his commendation is written to the Colossians, please note these are qualities that should be present and active and flowing from our Christian lives today—would you say your life is characterized by faith, hope, and love? And with consideration of the relevance of Scripture, Paul's initial target audience lived 2000 years ago, but his writing here is no less pertinent for us today! Forget church growth plans and seminars, Friends, let's just exemplify faith, love and hope in our hearts and lives, flowing from the grace of God—let's make them our currency, and we will not be able to keep people away from our Christian communities!

You see, word had gotten out, and it had gotten to Paul in prison, through Epaphras and likely Timothy, that the Colossian church knew how to love and express that love in quite a contagious fashion. Because of it, spiritual fruit was being born—other folks were hearing and trusting in the gospel of Jesus Christ.

Well over a year ago, through a 'chance' meeting at my local gym, I met a young college football player, and began discussing Fellowship of Christian Athletes with him. (I describe him a little in the Philippians writings as well) In short order, he became one of our leaders at Sunday Night Live, the weekly San Clemente High group I lead. If you were to ask the students to use one word to describe 'Big Dave', it would be **love**. Actually, I have never met anyone quite like him, so willing to embrace with a hug and a big smile, so willing to give of himself from the love he has and lives for God. It is contagious . . .it spreads when he is in the room. I think he fits Paul's description of *faith and love from the faith he has* . . .When I am around it, I want to be swept up in it, I want to become like him, I want others to feel and know the love that comes from faith in Christ and the hope we share in him. Yup, Paul, I get the beautiful trio of faith, love and hope . . .I've felt it and seen it in action.

*Epaphras was a preacher of the gospel to the people in Colosse; he brought news of the church, and its goings-on to Paul, while he was imprisoned in Rome.

From: Christine DiGiacomo, espressocd@cox.net

Subject: For this reason . . .we pray. Colossians 1.3-9

"We always thank God, the Father of our Lord Jesus Christ, when we pray for you . . .since the day we heard about you, we have not stopped praying for you. We continually ask God to fill you with the knowledge of his will through all the wisdom and understanding that the Spirit gives . . ." from verses 3-9

Paul puts such a premium on prayer, mentioning his prayer for the Colossians several times in just these few verses. Prayer.

I have to stop right here . . .honestly gripped by several situations, and several Christian brothers, wondering how to proceed in life. I believe at the heart of their inquiries is this heartfelt sentiment:

IF I AM TO GO ON, I MUST HEAR FROM GOD!

Accordingly, I believe the question is this: how do I live as though my life has meaning?

How do I proceed on that meaning as though I can HEAR in prayer, as well as speak forth my own needs?

MY FRIENDS, prayer must be both—an issuing forth of our personal thoughts, requests and seeking after God, and also a time of asking and listening, that the Spirit of God might come and fill our minds, hearts and beings with himself . . .which include his thoughts and plans for us . . .his very being that we might be one with another, even as we are One with him.

Let's think about prayer for a moment . . .and might I ask you, 'Do you pray?' 'Of course, I pray; really, I pray all the time.'

How do you pray? 'Well, I guess, I'm regularly shooting up one-liners throughout the day—'

What do you say? Usually, something like 'God, help me with _____; or thank you for _____ . . .I kinda have an open line going all the time.' That's a great start.

More Americans, more people 'round this world will pray this week than will exercise, drive a car, have sex, or go to work, according to Gallup polls. Nine in ten pray regularly, and yet most would say they aren't really satisfied with their prayer life. Some are not sure their prayers are being heard—maybe they aren't praying the right way or for the right things. Others think that prayer should be a conversation with God, and yet they never hear God say anything, and feel frustrated. Still others see their friends' prayers answered, but can't remember answered prayer themselves. Then there is the whole matter of getting distracted while praying—well really, I guess there are some things at issue here, aren't there?

"Prayer is an expression of who we are . . .We are a living incompleteness. We are a gap, an emptiness that calls for fulfillment," Thomas Merton said. I think Merton was right. In order to be complete, we need to be filled up with God, and that comes primarily through connectedness with him through communication. How many prayers have gone unanswered in your life because you never prayed them? Our Lord's brother said, 'We do not have, because we do not _____.' James 4.3.

Prayer connects us with God, it moves the hand of God, and changes us. It increases our faith, and helps us become who God wants us to be . . .but 'you know what? In order for it to be effective, in order for it to be powerful, it requires more than just one-liners throughout our day. It requires some 'set apart' time, when God is our sole focus, not just something we fit in with whatever we are doing. Prayer reminds me that he is God, and I am not. For this reason . . .we pray.

From: Christine DiGiacomo, espressocd@cox.net

Subject: My Prayer for You. Colossians 1.3-14

I hear regularly from folks round the world who need to know they are 'on track', who need to know that God is looking out for them, loving and guiding them . . .

Consider these words from a Kenyan brother, quoting in full, "Christine, how is the new year? I gain a lot from your teaching and my day would not be complete without a reading from you. I look at how things are happening to me, think about what has happened to me—there is a reason why all are happening. 1) I reap a bad harvest; I plant much, but harvest little. 2) My business income disappears as though I put it in a pocket filled with holes. 3) I look for much and get so little. Please assist me to find the answer; there is a reason why these things are happening."

When life is difficult, when things are not going as planned . . .what to do? I suppose my default setting prompts me to pray. So allow me to personalize Paul's words to the Colossians, turning them into a prayer for God's people, a prayer for you.

My brothers and sisters, I thank God, the Father of our Lord Jesus Christ, when I pray for you, because I have heard of your faith in Christ Jesus. *Friends, do you know what it is like to share in the bond of faith we have and experience in Jesus?* In truth, we share in the faith and love that spring from the hope stored up for us in heaven, which comes from the true message of the gospel that has come to you. And then I see how the gospel is bearing fruit and growing throughout the whole world—all because you understand God's grace, and have made yourselves available to share it with others. Yes, I see your words of encouragement on Facebook, All About God, and in personal e-mails . . . I see how God is at work in you!

For this reason, *I will not stop praying for you.* I will continually ask God to fill you with the knowledge of his will through all the wisdom and understanding that the Spirit gives, so that you may live a life worthy of the Lord and please him in every way: bearing fruit in every good work, growing in the knowledge of God, being strengthened with all power according to his glorious might so that you may have great endurance and patience, and giving joyful thanks to the Father, who has qualified you to share in the inheritance of his holy people in the kingdom of light. Amen.

To my Kenyan brother – besides praying for you, in an effort to help you assess what is happening in your life, I must humbly ask you what I ask of myself—in Paul's words, are you 'living a life worthy of the Lord and pleasing him in every way'? Are you bearing fruit for God? Are you growing in the knowledge of God?' Here's the thing—**our lives must be all one piece**.

Never forget that God has rescued us from the dominion of darkness and brought us into the kingdom of the Son he loves, in whom we have redemption, the forgiveness of sins. Amen. *Taken from Colossians 1.3-14*

From: Christine DiGiacomo, espressocd@cox.net

Subject: Walk like this. Colossians 1.3-14

She was sitting at my kitchen table, having come along with a couple of her sports chums, with Bible and notebook in hand, ready to be taught. Dani was young and brand new to the Christian faith, but she wanted so badly to do the right thing. At one point, she asked me for a list of sins, so as to be able to make wise choices with her life, and honor God. Wow! Somehow it seemed like she had been inoculated with Paul's sentiments as he wrote to the Colossian believers: "Walk (live and conduct yourselves) in a manner worthy of the Lord, fully pleasing to him and desiring to please him in all things, bearing fruit in every good work and steadily growing and increasing in and by the knowledge of God [with fuller, deeper, and clearer insight, acquaintance, and recognition]." Verse is from the Amplified Bible.

What does it mean to 'walk in a manner worthy of the Lord'? Brought to mind were the words from the Old Bible, as my mama used to call it, "What does the Lord require of you? To act justly, to love mercy, and to walk humbly with the Lord your God."[1] But when I put pen to paper this morning, and looked at the larger passage we have been considering, perhaps the clues to 'worthy walking' lie within these very same verses.

"God, what is walking in a manner worthy of you?" I asked. The answer starts with faith in Christ Jesus[2], from verse 4. We cannot know God, walk with God, or walk in a manner worthy of him, without faith in Jesus. It all starts there; without Jesus, 'faggetaboutit'. It is Jesus who delivers us from darkness[3]; it is Jesus who redeems us; it is Jesus who forgives us of our sins[4]. When we choose to accept Jesus, God pours out his love into our hearts by the Holy Spirit, whom he has given us,[5] and then we are filled with the Spirit.

'So, how do I know if I am filled with the Spirit?' you ask. 'Mostly by the contents of your heart ~> which will then overflow to your actions. Three things usually characterize the life of a person filled with the Holy Spirit: *love* for God and others, and *joy*; a desire to *serve* others from the gifts God bestowed upon you when you came to know him,[6] a *passion to share Christ* with those who do not know him. Having a soft heart toward God, and a strong desire to please him are indicators that the Spirit is in you as well.

Paul told us to be continually filled with the Holy Spirit.[7] Personally, I know that the Holy Spirit is with me, but there are times I do not *feel* his presence. When that is the case, I think of whether or not I have done anything to grieve my God, confess it and ask forgiveness, and then I ask God to fill me anew, to fill me afresh with his Holy Spirit.

These are the things that help us to know that when we walk like this we are walking in a manner worthy of the Lord.

1 Micah 6.8
2 Colossians 1.4
3 Colossians 1.13
4 Colossians 1.14
5 Romans 5.5
6 1 Corinthians 12
7 Ephesians 5.18

From: Christine DiGiacomo, <u>espressocd@cox.net</u>

Subject: Jesus Christ. . .Who He Is.
Colossians 1.15-18

During the recent winter vacation, I accompanied my son, Dylan – 17, to Scotsdale, Arizona, for a big high school soccer tournament. Besides seeing some great soccer, and an area of the country I had not before seen, I also had the opportunity to spend time with some other team parents I had not known very well. One afternoon between games, I went to lunch with two of the other mothers—one who was born and raised in Japan. When she learned a little about me, she quietly said, 'I am a good candidate to be a Christian.' 'Oh, why is that?' I asked, taking a bite of one very great taco. 'Well because I went all of my school years to a Catholic school, and I know a lot about Jesus.' 'Well then, why don't you believe in him?' I asked. 'Oh I do, but I don't want to abandon my other gods. See in my country, we have the Shinto religion, and we believe in many gods. We pray to different gods for individual things such as fertility, weddings, and at the time of death—things like that. I don't want to miss out on those things,' and then she lowered her eyelids and rather demurely chuckled.

To most Western Christians, the idea of many gods seems foreign, at the very least. But in practice, I think our culture has become rather polytheistic, whether we know or recognize the reality. Oh, we don't want to offend, and we must be open-minded(!), so we think that Jesus-plus-other things can't be too harmful. . .right? You know what I'm saying–Jesus + positive thinking . . . Jesus + some Buddhist principles . . . Jesus + New Age beliefs . . .etc., then, we've got all the bases covered too, just like my new soccer mom friend. 'Of course, I believe Jesus was a great moral teacher!'

However, it does not work, because that kind of thinking is antithetical to a Holy God. Have you read the Ten Commandments lately? The first one reads: "You shall have no other gods before me." No idols, no bowing down, no worship of another god . . .period. Why? Because God said, I, the Lord your God, am a jealous God[1]. And then of course, here in Colossians 1, Paul goes on to explain the supreme position of the Son of God, in relation to God the Father, beginning in verse 15. . .

"Now Christ is the visible expression of the invisible God. He existed before creation began, for it was through him that every thing was made, whether spiritual or material, seen or unseen. Through him, and for him, also, were created power and dominion, ownership and authority. In fact, every single thing was created through, and for him. He is both the first principle and the upholding principle of the whole scheme of creation." *J.B. Phillips New Testament* Colossians 1.15-18

Hmmm . . . No other gods before him. Jesus, Son of God, Creator of all things—external and internal, visible and invisible – he who has always been . . .equal with God the Father and the Holy Spirit . . .he who says, 'You shall have no other gods before me.' Jesus plus nothing.

And Paul goes on to say that besides creating all things, Jesus also redeemed us. "For God in all his fullness was pleased to live in Christ, and . . .now he has reconciled you to himself through the death of Christ in his physical body. As a result, he has brought you into his own presence, and you are holy and blameless."[2]

Oh don't you see, Friends, Jesus, who he is . . . well, he is fully God, God the Creator, God incarnate, and the perfect One given for us. We must never add something to Jesus; it must never be Jesus – plus – anything else. Nor can we ever say he was just a great teacher. Realize, "You can shut him up for a fool, you can spit at him and kill him as a demon; or you can fall at his feet and call him Lord and God. But let us not come up with any patronizing nonsense about his being a great human teacher. He has not left that open to us. He did not intend to."[3]

1 Exodus 20.3-5
2 Colossians 1.22
3 C.S. Lewis, Mere Christianity

From: Christine DiGiacomo, espressocd@cox.net

Subject: No Adulteration . . .in Jesus.
Colossians 1.15-23

Pray with me: O God, and author of Scripture, this part of Paul's letter that we have been studying is packed with such powerful theology, and the right ordering of things in we who confess your name. Please convey it's meaning to our hearts and minds this day. Amen.

Do you remember when you came to know Christ . . . when all things were new?

Do you remember what it felt like to have a new beginning, being cleansed of your sin? Do you remember the feeling that came upon you with the knowledge that you would never, ever be alone again? Do you remember the peace that settled upon you, when you devoted yourself to Jesus? Burdens rolled away, fears were quieted, worries quelled, because the very God of the Universe had made himself real to you! Remember? Truly, the conversion experience is an unparalleled one.

But in Colosse, the newness was wearing off for some folks, and the influence of false teachers was adulterating their living out of Christianity. You see, they were confused about their physical bodies, thinking that their physical lives were separate from their spiritual lives, which lead to confusion and false teaching about how they should live—the influence of the Gnostics. While they followed Jesus' teaching, the Colossian believers were also trying to include Greek philosophy and Eastern mysticism. They were practicing angel worship, thinking of the angels as advocates before the Father[2]. And finally, Jewish legalism was seeping in again—rules and regulations were beginning to define their practice of faith. From prison, in great concern, it was Paul's highest desire to set things straight for the young Christians, and so he wrote clearly and simply:

"Christ is the visible image of the invisible God.
He existed before anything was created and is supreme over all creation, for through him God created everything . . .
Christ is also the head of the church, which is his body.
He is the beginning, supreme over all who rise from the dead.
So he is first in everything.

133

For God in all his fullness was pleased to live in Christ,
and through him God reconciled everything to himself . . .
by means of Christ's blood on the cross.
This includes you who were once far away from God.
He has reconciled you to himself through the death of Christ in his physical body.
As a result, he has brought you into his own presence,
and you are holy and blameless as you stand before him without a single fault.
But you must continue to believe this truth and stand firmly in it.
Don't drift away from the assurance you received when you heard the Good News.
The Good News has been preached all over the world, and
I, Paul, have been appointed as God's servant to proclaim it."
From Colossians 1.15-23

What a treatise! So thorough, so deep – Jesus, God of very God; Creator and Reconciler. Because of the cross, we can be holy and pure again—through Jesus ONLY, not plus anything else, and not diluted by anyone else. Beware of other add-ins or add-ons. Sift everything by the Scripture. Test it and check it for yourself . . . be wise. Because, like the Colossians, we live in an age when false teaching is sliding into the church. Take care that there be no adulteration . . .remain in Jesus.

*–Steve Znachko

From: Christine DiGiacomo, espressocd@cox.net

Subject: Stay the Course. Colossians 1.23

But you must continue to believe this truth and stand firmly in it. Don't drift away from the assurance you received when you heard the Good News. Colossians 1.23, NLT

Last week, I shared verses 3 through 14 with the high school student leaders, mentioning the premium Paul put on <u>praying</u> for the Colossian believers—stressing to them that we must be praying for one another. There were 21 of the teens, and they seemed to be following me, taking it in, some even making notes, but I can never be sure, until somehow a scripture or lesson comes back around. Well, it did . . .in short order.

Some of the best text messages I get from these much-loved students of mine come late at night, when their day is finally winding down, and I am already long asleep. This one was from a football player, a junior, newly transformed by the power of the Gospel – truly! It read: "Hey Christine, it's Jamo, I was wondering if you had any prayer requests . . ." 'Oh, my goodness,' I thought. 'He got it!' I responded, asking that he pray for my oldest child, who is far from God. 'And how about you?' I queried. "That I will stay strong in my faith and bring glory to God on campus," he texted. 'Yes, Lord,' I looked upward, 'he really got it. And Lord, thank you for Jamo—thanks for what you are doing in him.'

Paul includes Jamo's admonition here in chapter one: "Continue in your faith, established and firm, and do not move from the hope held out in the gospel." In essence, Paul is saying, "Christ Follower: Stay the Course." He had told the Corinthians, 'Be strong, immovable in your faith . . .'[1] "He who called you is faithful"[2] and 'he will strengthen and protect from the evil one.'[3] Christian, we are to stay the course because God is faithful, and it is what he asks of us.

Besides, people are watching us. People are watching you and me when we go through difficulties in life. How do we fare? Are we running scared or trusting, believing that the God who has got 'the whole world in his hands' has us, too. We say that we trust God, but do we trust him with our tough circumstances, with our heartaches, and in the midst of our trials? Do we trust that—no matter what—his heart toward us is good? We bring glory to God when we truly trust him.

How to stay the course, or 'stay at your post'? I close with this passage from 1 Timothy, with more to follow tomorrow—

"Stay at your post reading Scripture, giving counsel, teaching. And that special gift of ministry you were given when the leaders of the church laid hands on you and prayed–keep that dusted off and in use. Cultivate these things. Immerse yourself in them. The people will all see you mature right before their eyes! Keep a firm grasp on both your character and your teaching. Don't be diverted. Just keep at it. Both you and those who hear you will experience salvation."[4]

Stay the course . . .stay strong in the Lord and in his mighty power.[5]

1–1 CORINTHIANS 15.58
2- 1 THESSALONIANS 5.24
3 – 2 THESSALONIANS 3.3
4 – 1 TIMOTHY 4.13-16, THE MESSAGE
5 – EPHESIANS 6.10

From: Christine DiGiacomo, espressocd@cox.net

Subject: How to Stay Faithful. Colossians 1.23.

Maintain a firm position in the faith, and do not allow your-selves to be shifted away from the hope of the Gospel. Colossians 1.23, J.B. Phillips

Most people place faith in something—be it God, Buddha, a Higher Power, or whatever—but in that faith, I have noticed, that the majority are not very faithful! It is not easy to remain faithful—living in this world just seems to leech godliness right out of us, does it not?

Yet, Paul said, "Be steadfast, immovable, always abounding in the work of the Lord, knowing that your toil is not in vain in the Lord."[1]

In short, when Paul tells us to 'be steadfast, immovable, always abounding in the work of the Lord,' he is saying, 'be faithful.' Be loyal. Constant.

Be faithful—the 'be' part is a verb, which implies action on our part.

It will take action to be faithful in this life. See, here's the thing—we are easily distracted, easily pulled away, though we would say we would surely die for God if we were asked!

How do weak human beings remain faithful?'

These verses from the heart and mind of David provide clues:
Blessed *is* the man **w**ho walks not in the counsel of the ungodly,

Nor stands in the path of sinners,
Nor sits in the seat of the scornful;

But his delight *is* in the law of the Lord,
And in His law he meditates day and night.

He shall be like a tree
Planted by the rivers of water,
That brings forth its fruit in its season,
Whose leaf also shall not wither;
And whatever he does shall prosper.[2]

Do you want to stay the course? <u>Choose your company wisely</u>, the psalmist advises; otherwise, they will pull you down, and pull you away. Paul said, "Do not be misled: Bad company corrupts good character."[3] How could it be any other way, really? It is short-sighted to think, 'we only go around once, so better live it up!' And life is fleeting and lacks significance compared to Heaven and eternity with God.

Second, <u>meditate on the Word</u> as though it were your only sustenance. It will make and keep you strong; take it in, and you will be like a tree whose roots go down very deep, drawing water into its very core; through it, you become what Paul said immovable. Through it, you will prosper. Get the Word through reading, studying, and by hearing inspired teaching from the Word of the Lord on the Lord's Day.

Third, remember that God is with you . . .always. It was not long ago that we studied Jesus' words in John: In this world you will have trouble. But take heart! I have overcome the world.[4]

No matter what you are facing, you do not face it alone.

And from the Old Bible, "Have I not commanded you? Be strong and courageous. Do not be terrified; do not be discouraged, for the LORD your God will be with you wherever you go."[5]

Finally, in order to stay the course, keep your eye on the finish line. "I focus on this one thing: Forgetting the past and looking forward to what lies ahead, I press on to reach the end of the race and receive the heavenly prize for which God, through Christ Jesus, is calling us."[6]

1 – 1 Corinthians 15.58
2 – Psalm 1.1-3
3 – 1 Corinthians 15.33
4 – John 16.33
5 – Joshua 1.9
6 – From Philippians 3

From: Christine DiGiacomo, espressocd@cox.net

Subject: Temptation and Staying the Course. Colossians 1.23

Maintain a firm position in the faith, and do not allow yourselves to be shifted away from the hope of the Gospel. J.B. Phillips

He always comes into the room quietly and takes a seat—whether at Fellowship of Christian Athletes, Sunday Night Live, or anywhere else. He is a junior and a basketball player, and he's the kinda' kid that just tries hard at everything. He's got a great big, genuine smile and is liked by all. For some reason, after seeing him the other night, I felt prompted to text him later, and ask how I could pray for him. When his class time permitted, he responded with, "I'm having trouble with temptation and have been praying about it. If you could too that would be awesome." I texted back, "I will . . .Thanks for being straight up."

That was Monday, and the exchange continues to replay itself in my head. I was honored by his honesty and trust; I was reminded that it is Scriptural to pray for others in the area of temptation, and I began thinking of the connection of 'staying the course' and standing strong in the face of temptation.

Temptation is a given in this life. All of us are tempted . . .and certainly, when giving in to temptation leads to sin, it hinders our relationship with God. Here's the question—from whence does temptation come?

And, does God tempt us?

If not . . .where does the temptation come from??

Let's go back to the beginning. Back in Genesis, we find the entrance of temptation[1]. . .which of course, by its very nature implies a choice, and that choice includes evil. Eve, and then Adam, could not stand up to the temptation put before them 'to really know', which the serpent told them they would, **if** they ate of the tree of knowledge . . .With the choice made by the first couple, the sin condition entered what had been a perfect world. (Notice that temptation came through an appeal to pride)

Does God send temptation our way? Hmmmm . . .consider this from James:

"No one, when tempted, should say, "I am being tempted by God"; for God cannot be tempted by evil and he himself tempts no one. But one is tempted by one's own desire, being lured and enticed by it; then, when that desire has conceived, it gives birth to sin, and that sin, when it is fully grown, gives birth to death."[2]

James is pretty clear that **God does not tempt anyone; *it is impossible for God to violate his own character***. Thomas a Kempis in his work, "The Temptation of Christ", written in 1441, has some keen insight on this critical topic.

The beginning of all evil temptations is an unstable mind and a small trust in God. Just as a ship without a helm is tossed about by the waves, so a person who lacks resolution and certainty is tossed about by temptations . . .temptations reveal who we are.

It is our own (individual) desires that entice. It is for this reason that what tempts you, may not tempt me, and vice versa. It is valuable to see that ***temptation is part of a process-***

>First, the *thought* is allowed to enter our minds~
>Second, the *imagination* is sparked by the thought~
>Third, we feel a sense of pleasure at the *fantasy*, and we entertain it~
>Fourth, and finally, *we engage* in the evil action, assenting to its urges.

Kempis admonishes us about thoughts of temptation,

"Meet them at the door as soon as they knock, and do not let them in."

We can overcome temptation with the help of the Holy Spirit. The Holy Spirit gives us the power to resist temptation . . .**if** we look to him. "The Lord knows how to deliver the godly out of temptation."[3]

God promises he will not allow us to be tempted beyond what we can bear—"but with the temptation will also make the way of escape, that you may be able to bear it."[4]

Hmmm . . .do you conduct yourself wisely, or do you flirt with temptation that will lead to sin by opening yourself up to it? James instructed, "Submit yourselves therefore to God. Resist the devil, and he will flee from you."[5]

Temptation – here's what to do: Pray for strength before and when you face it, do not flirt with it, and like a Kempis said, 'when temptation knocks on the door, meet it at the door, and do not let it in'! 'Something to think about before you AND me are knee-deep in the muck. God, grant us your strength. Amen.

1 – Genesis 3.1
2 – James 1.13-15
3 – 2 Peter 2.9
4–1 Corinthians 10.13
5 – James 4.7

From: Christine DiGiacomo, espressocd@cox.net

Subject: Zooming back out . . .Colossians 1.22-29

Today, we are zooming back out, and looking at context as well-in verses 22-29. Our beloved Paul writes from prison to the believers in Colosse:

"But now he has reconciled you by Christ's physical body through death to present you holy in his sight, without blemish and free from accusation—23 **if** you continue in your faith, established and firm, and do not move from the hope held out in the gospel. This is the gospel that you heard and that has been proclaimed to every creature under heaven, and of which I, Paul, have become a servant." *Friends, please note with me the "if" at the start of verse 23. You and I are the reason Christ died . . .so that when we stand before the Father, at the close of our earthly lives, God will see us as redeemed and holy. Hence the reason it is paramount that we remain faithful to Jesus Christ.*

"Now I rejoice in what I am suffering for you . . ." *Paul suffered mocking, floggings, multiple imprisonments, stoning, hunger, and loneliness, all for preaching the gospel. And he says here 'he rejoices in it!'* He continues, "and I fill up in my flesh what is still lacking in regard to Christ's afflictions, for the sake of his body, which is the church."

And then Paul says something about himself, which has application to you and to me: "I have become its servant by the commission God gave me to present to you the word of God in its fullness . . ."

You and I have been given this same commission. Indeed, we have been commissioned to share the love of Jesus, the Good News of the Gospel with those around us. Why, don't you remember some of Jesus' last words—just before he ascended into Heaven—"You shall receive power when the Holy Spirit comes upon you, and **you will be my witnesses** . . ." *Acts 1.8*

"I have become its servant by the commission God gave me to present to you the word of God in its fullness—the mystery that has been kept hidden for ages and generations, but is now disclosed to the Lord's people. To them God has chosen to make known among the Gentiles the glorious riches of this mystery, which is Christ in you, the hope of glory.

He is the one we proclaim, admonishing and teaching everyone with all wisdom, so that we may present everyone fully mature in Christ. To this end I strenuously contend with all the energy Christ so powerfully works in me." *Picture Paul with me: If he were a lone actor being shown on the set in his dank and dirty prison cell, telling his audience, even reminding himself, and reaffirming to the God he loves his call, his very reason for living . . .at this point, the lights would dim, and we the audience would spring to our feet with thunderous applause and shouts!*

Such brave commitment, such passion that moves Paul, one rarely witnesses in a lifetime, but when he or she does take it in, it evokes a visceral response . . .and may I submit to you, that it calls for some introspection? I ask myself, 'how committed am I to what God commissioned me to do—simply telling others what I know and have experienced of Jesus, and his love?' And how about you, do you ever take a risk and tell someone 'there is a God who loves you more than you can ever think or imagine'?

When Jesus said, 'be my witnesses', he was talking to some small group of his followers on a hilltop, and Paul was not even there. Jesus was also talking to you and me, saying something like, 'come on, just tell them how I've loved you.'

From: Christine DiGiacomo, espressocd@cox.net

Paul, A Life Well Lived. Colossians 2.1-5

Libraries of respected leaders, managers and savvy busi-nesspeople usually contain biographies of people who have led meaningful, purposeful lives. That is because reading about the driving force in others' lives is both inspirational and motiva-tional. In fact, the study of A LIFE WELL LIVED oft galvanizes folks to take action in their own lives. 'Your attention? Otherwise, what? Otherwise, you get to be 80 years old and you look back, and say, 'so I don't think I made the world a better place by my years here . . .and really, I don't think I impacted too many people for good either.'

The Bible is an encyclopedia of quite a few impressive biog-raphies, which is one more compelling reason to study the Scripture. (Honestly, I have never thought of it quite that way, until now) Here at the start of Colossians 2, we find ourselves getting to know the heartbeat of one Paul the Apostle, a.k.a. Saul of Tarsus. We remember from past studies that his pedigree was of stellar Jewish stock, and he was also a Roman citizen; he was educated by probably the world's most highly regarded first-century rabbi, Gamaliel, in Jerusalem.

Whatever he set his mind to, he did it with everything in him—he was passionate! When he persecuted the Christians, as recorded in the early part of the book of Acts, he wanted them prosecuted to the fullest extent of Roman law, endeavoring to protect his precious Judaism. But when confronted with TRUTH in the person of Jesus Christ on the Damascus direction,[1] Paul then transitioned from a life driven by the Law to one transformed by grace. So in love with his Savior was he, that he seemed to make it his life's mission to fulfill Acts 1, verse 8, all on his own: But you will receive power when the Holy Spirit comes on you; and you will be my witnesses in Jerusalem, and in all Judea and Samaria, and to the ends of the earth. He introduced people to the Good News of the Gospel wherever he went, and then set out on his first missionary journey some 10 years after his own conversion, establishing churches as he went.

Imprisoned (likely in Rome) for preaching of Christ, he writes to Colosse and includes the town of Laodicea, located a little more than ten miles away—wanting his letter to be read aloud to the believers in both communities. Confined, Paul agonizes in prayer for his fellow brothers in Christ, revealing his great affinity for them.

Take a look with me at Colossians 2, verses 1–5: "I want you to know how much I am struggling for you and for those at Laodicea, and for all who have not met me personally. My purpose is that they may be encouraged in heart and united in love, so that they may have the full riches of complete understanding, in order that they may know the mystery of God, namely, Christ, in whom are hidden all the treasures of wisdom and knowledge. I tell you this so that no one may deceive you by fine-sounding arguments. For though I am absent from you in body, I am present with you in spirit and delight to see how orderly you are and how firm your faith in Christ is.[2]

In these few short verses, he encourages the Christians, and states his purpose: that others may be united in love and have full knowledge of Christ, and remain firm in that faith.

As I think of it, Paul was probably just a few years older than me when he wrote these words; I can see no greater purpose for my life than that: **my purpose is that they may be encouraged in heart, united in love, have full knowledge of Christ, and stand firm in the faith**. Thank you, my brother; thank you, my mentor, Paul.

1 – probably somewhere around 33-36 A.D.
2 – New International Version 1984

From: Christine DiGiacomo, espressocd@cox.net

Subject: Good, Solid Instruction. Colossians 2.6-23

Paul is writing from a shepherd's heart to his beloved flock, passionate about their faith in Jesus Christ, unswerving in his desire that they 'get it right':

"And now, just as you accepted Christ Jesus as your Lord, you must continue to follow him. **Let your roots grow down into him**, and **let your lives be built on him**. **Then your faith will grow strong** in the truth you were taught, and **you will overflow with thankfulness**.

Don't let anyone capture you with empty philosophies and high-sounding nonsense that come from human thinking and from the spiritual powers of this world, rather than from Christ. For in Christ lives all the fullness of God in a human body. So you also are complete through your union with Christ, who is the head over every ruler and authority.

When you came to Christ, you were "circumcised," but not by a physical procedure. Christ performed a spiritual circumcision—the cutting away of your sinful nature. For you were buried with Christ when you were baptized. And with him you were raised to new life because you trusted the mighty power of God, who raised Christ from the dead.

You were dead because of your sins and because your sinful nature was not yet cut away. Then God made you alive with Christ, for he forgave all your sins. He canceled the record of the charges against you and took it away by nailing it to the cross. In this way, he disarmed the spiritual rulers and authorities. He shamed them publicly by his victory over them on the cross.

So don't let anyone condemn you for what you eat or drink, or for not celebrating certain holy days or new moon ceremonies or Sabbaths. For these rules are only shadows of the reality yet to come. And Christ himself is that reality. Don't let anyone condemn you by insisting on pious self-denial or the worship of angels, saying they have had visions about these things. Their sinful minds have made them proud, and they are not connected to Christ, the head of the body. For he holds the whole body together with its joints and ligaments, and it grows as God nourishes it.

You have died with Christ, and he has set you free from the spiritual powers of this world. So why do you keep on following the rules of the world, such as, "Don't handle! Don't taste! Don't touch!"? Such rules are mere human teachings about things that deteriorate as we use them. These rules may seem wise because they require strong devotion, pious self-denial, and severe bodily discipline. But they provide no help in conquering a person's evil desires."

Again I say:

And now, just as you accepted Christ Jesus as your Lord, you must continue to follow him. **Let your roots grow down into him**, and **let your lives be built on him**. **Then your faith will grow strong** in the truth you were taught, and **you will overflow with thankfulness**.

Friends, don't let anyone or anything pull you away from the love and truth of Jesus Christ.

From: Christine DiGiacomo, espressocd@cox.net

Subject: Set yourself on things Above. Colossians 3.2

Set your minds on things above, not on earthly things.

Regularly, I consult my Mac dictionary to see full descriptions of familiar words; in fact, I just looked up the word 'set.' Wow, what a highly utilized word! The first definition of the verb 'set' is simply PUT, LAY OR STAND (SOMETHING) IN A SPECIFIED PLACE OR POSITION. Notice with me that this definition employs <u>intention</u>. Since, then, you have been raised with Christ, set your hearts on things above . . .or as we recall from chapter one, since we are endeavoring to 'live a life worthy of the Lord'[1], what we set our minds on is critical. I will go so far as to say, <u>what we choose to think about defines us</u>.

Set your minds on things above, not on earthly things. **Learn to think God's thoughts after him**. The whole notion of *thinking God's thoughts after him* has me riveted! Of course, it is the ULTIMATE in thinking. After all, God is omniscient—he possesses all knowledge, he knows everything perfectly and eternally—all things which can be known, past, present, and future . . .

Where to start with learning to think God's thoughts? Hmmm . . .well, let's think about it. First of course would be our acknowledgment that, as he said, "My thoughts are not your thoughts, neither are your ways my ways, as the heavens are higher than the earth, so are my ways higher than your ways and my thoughts than your thoughts."[2] Beginning with the understanding that he is God and we are not, we put the highest value on his thinking and ways, and we earnestly desire to know them. As one very intelligent person said, "I want to know God's thoughts . . .the rest are details." WHO SAID THAT?[3]

In the beginning, God . . .and since the creation of the world, God's invisible qualities—his eternal power and divine nature—have been clearly seen, being understood from what has been made.[4] **Ponder, study the Creator**, who he is, and what he is like. I said to my dear friend, Heidi, the other day, as we were remarking about the beauty of God's handiwork, particularly as we were looking at birds and colorful flowers, "If someone were to paint these colors God used in this flower, we would think he took license!" Friend, look closely at the intense color of an orchid or lily, breathe in the fragrance of a gardenia, take time to note the array of colors in the sunset over the water . . .the mind of a brilliant Creator spoke them into being.

How to know God's mind? **Get to know his Son**. Think of the love Jesus taught and modeled as we just studied through the pages of John's gospel. Think of the strength and courage of Jesus Christ, and the brilliance of his mind. How to know God's thoughts? Read the printed Word of God—his love letter to us, and communicate with him—pray. Talk to him, and <u>ask him to speak to you</u>. **Listen**. **Create space for him to inhabit with you**. <u>Long to feel his presence</u>. 'He will be found by you when you seek him with all your heart.'[5] Set your minds on things above . . .by seeking to think God's thoughts after him for they are the highest of thoughts.

Setting your mind on things above takes training, and training of any kind that is worthwhile is hard work. People will train for two years to run a marathon, though it seems training our bodies is much more popular in our culture than training our minds, (particularly toward godliness). Paul did not back away from the challenge: "I discipline my body like an athlete, training it to do what it should . . ."[6] To be sure, training the mind takes discipline, but the effort is more than worthwhile! Setting our minds on things above isn't overly complicated, but it is a discipline, and will need to be cultivated and refined. I love the word and the notion of discipline, because it paves the way for us to become who we were meant to be.

1 – Colossians 1.10
2 – Isaiah 55.8-9
3 – Albert Einstein
4 – Romans 1.20
5 – Jeremiah 29.13
6 – 1 Corinthians 9.27

From: Christine DiGiacomo, espressocd@cox.net

Subject: Are you Alive . . .really? Colossians 3.1-4

Since you have been raised to new life with Christ . . .
Jesus said, I came that they may have life, and have it abundantly . . .then he was crucified and rose again—defeating death—all to offer us that most abundant life. Paul starts this passage with "Since," implying that a transaction has occurred. In this case, the transaction was our acceptance of Christ's offer of new life. Take a look: *Since you have been raised to new life with Christ, set your sights on the realities of heaven, where Christ sits in the place of honor at God's right hand. Think about the things of heaven, not the things of earth. For you died to this life, and your real life is hidden with Christ in God. And when Christ, who is your life, is revealed to the whole world, you will share in all his glory. Colossians 3.1-4*
Life in Christ includes forgiveness of sin, Jesus as the Leader of our lives, and the promise of forever with him. Yes, life in Christ is indeed eternal, but most of us operate as though it begins when our bodies die. Think about it. But what it really means is abundant fullness of life even now. You see, when we assume our new lives in Christ, it means we will live eternally with him, but are also now fully alive in him, just as Paul himself said, "for to me to live is Christ."[1] It means defeat of sin when we apprehend our new identities in him. Our exalted position in Christ (that Paul talks about here) is not a hypothetical thing or a goal for which we strive. It is an accomplished fact.[2] It is part of the "It is finished".
Let's stop here for a moment – perhaps that "since" assumes a contract you have not entered into—a relationship that is not yours; what I mean is, perhaps you do not have new life in Christ, perhaps you just have religion. Think of that sad state of affairs: religion without the truth of relationship with your Savior, Jesus Christ. Then again, perhaps you profess belief in a god, several gods, or even Jesus, but you have never entered into relationship with him. After all, James said, even the demons believe.[3]

Your individual decision to enter into a relationship with Christ is the single most important decision you will ever make. It not only impacts this moment in time, but your 'forever'. While there is no one right way to express your heart, there are a few things to think of: Admit you are a sinner, and want to be forgiven of your sins; Believe that Jesus Christ, Son of God, paid for your sins on the cross because of his great love for you; Come to him, and offer yourself to his leadership. Pray to him, and tell him these things. He will take up residence in your life—you will never be without him again. God promises, "Never will I leave you, never will I forsake you."[4]

And now, you have entered new life.

1 Philippians 1.21
2 Warren Wiersbe, NT Bible Commentary
3 James 2.19
4 Hebrews 13.5

From: Christine DiGiacomo, espressocd@cox.net

Subject: Quality of Life? Colossians 3.1

Since you have been raised to new life with Christ . . .

I read something the other day that really made me think: Life in Christ includes forgiveness of sin, Jesus as the Leader of our lives, and the promise of forever with him. Yes, life in Christ is indeed eternal, but <u>most of us operate as though it begins when our bodies die</u>. Think about it. But what it really means is abundant <u>fullness of life</u> even now. You see, when we assume our new lives in Christ, it means we will live eternally with him, but are also <u>now fully alive in him</u>, just as Paul himself said, "for to me to live is Christ."[1] It means defeat of sin when we apprehend our new identities in him. Our exalted position in Christ is not a hypothetical thing or a goal for which we strive. It is an accomplished fact.[2] It was part of the "It is finished".

Yup, it made me think, because I wrote it. Now may I ask you, 'what is the quality of your new life in Christ?' Paul said, we "have been raised to new life in Christ" . . .but it seems that so many of us Christ followers are not really alive, not really living the abundant life. And since Jesus said that is what he came for – that we may have abundant life[3]—then what's our problem?

Yuck. Our problem is too much yuck. We have yuck that we carry around with us. Many of us aren't even aware of it, or think 'that's just the way it is' . . .'just the way I roll' . . .or 'cuz of what I've been through . . .' Hmmm, so I guess that Jesus' ability to provide his children with abundant, joy-filled living is limited. Is that we are saying here? But, but Paul told the Roman Christians that in all things, **we are more than conquerors.**[4] Was Paul making grand claims he did not believe or live? No, Paul knew from experience. He wrote, 'in all things, we are more than conquerors' to the Romans before these words to the Colossians about living new life in Christ. He could say he was a conqueror; he could talk about new, true life in Christ, because he had experienced it. 'Because his life had been easy? Of course not! We know that Paul faced every trial known to man.

I used to be friends with an army vet who lived off his pension, and just worked out all day long. At 39 years of age, Tom was quite a physical specimen—6 ft., 6 inches tall, 202 pounds, and just two percent body fat. One number on his daily routine was running through thick beach sand, with a 75-pound rucksack fastened to a shoulder harness, dragging through the sand. What an image! It was hard work and a lot of strain on Tom to run fast with that dragging through the sand behind him.

Under normal, everyday circumstances you are not meant to go through life, dragging heavy weight behind you. Christian, you aren't meant to have a rucksack of yuck, weighing you down, making life seem like a chore, stealing your joy, making you bitter, or keeping you from contentment.

"Search me, O God," the psalmist prayed, and then invited God to give him a pure heart. Do you want to get rid of your rucksack? Now's the time. *The Lord is good, and his mercy endures forever.*[6] He is waiting to take your rucksack, and give you newness of life in him . . .really.

1–Philippians 1.21
2–Warren Wiersbe, NT Bible Commentary
3 – John 10.10
4 – Romans 8.37
5 – Psalm 139.23
6 – Psalm 106.1

From: Christine DiGiacomo, espressocd@cox.net

Subject: Raised to New Life. Colossians 3.1-4

In November, two students approached me and asked if I would baptize them. Sister and brother, (junior and senior in high school), it was an interesting request, since I had not taught on baptism at Fellowship of Christian Athletes or Sunday Night Live, and they had not been raised in church, so why make such a request? The answer was simple: they wanted to obey Christ's example and also make public their commitments to follow him. In truth, baptism symbolizes what Paul was teaching in these verses:

Since you have been raised to new life with Christ, set your sights on the realities of heaven, where Christ sits in the place of honor at God's right hand. Think about the things of heaven, not the things of earth. For you died to this life, and your real life is hidden with Christ in God. And when Christ, who is your life, is revealed to the whole world, you will share in all his glory. Colossians 3.1-4

Baptism in Paul's day was different than is common today. It was adult baptism. (Infant baptism did not begin until around A.D. 200.) In the early church, baptism was connected with confession of faith. Baptism was usually total immersion, which symbolized being buried and when coming out of the water, rising from the grave. Symbolically, <u>baptism was like dying and rising again</u>. The man died to one kind of life and rose to another; he died to the old life of sin and rose to the new life of grace.

For you died to this life. . .and
    you have been raised to new life with Christ.

Well, word got out, and another student approached me, and asked to be baptized, and then another . . .and we picked a baptism date. I met with the students on campus ahead of time, to be certain of their commitments to Jesus, and talk about what baptism is, and what it is not. It is not baptism into a denomination, or membership in any church; it does not 'save' anyone, but rather is the demonstration of what has already taken place within the heart of an individual. And it symbolizes death to bondage of sin and rebirth to a new life.

On a cold, clear Sunday afternoon in December—just two days before Christmas—folks assembled at our locals' beach, Riviera, ready to participate in the faith commitments of 10 young adults. Two sets of siblings, in which Big Dave and I baptized brother first; then the brother would assist me in lowering his younger sister into the cold Pacific waters, only to raise her back up again, as the crowd on the beach exploded in cheers! So beautiful . . .so many teary eyes on the beach of onlookers. It truly was a joyful experience, a lovely demonstration of the newness of life Jesus offers those who would come after him . . . so amazing indeed.

For you died to this life . . .and
you have been raised to new life with Christ.

From: Christine DiGiacomo, espressocd@cox.net

Subject: L'Chaim! – To Life! To Freedom!
Colossians 3.1

Since you have been raised to new life in Christ . . .

You turned around to see what was holding you back, what was weighing you down, and you discovered you have been dragging a heavy burden, perhaps unaware until now. But when Christ offers you new life, he offers to take those burdens from you. In trade, he wants to give you a new heart, healed from ways the world has hurt you.

When you picked up your rucksack, (referenced in our Philippian study as well) ready to be honest with yourself, what did you find inside?

>GUILT over things that make you feel bad about yourself? Your head and heart do not operate at full capacity because you are constantly hearing in your head, 'yeah, well you failed there . . .' 'you're never gonna do it right, you'll never be good enough . . .'
>FAILURE TO FORGIVE, or maybe even SPECIFIC BITTERNESSES?
>BROKEN HEART, maybe by past pain from people, events, or relationships from which you never healed? Maybe things like child abuse, parental neglect, being the child of an alcoholic, an ugly divorce . . .
>UNMET EXPECTATIONS you placed in other people, like maybe your spouse, or your employer, or God? It leaves you constantly feeling defensive, skeptical of others' motives, perhaps a little self-centered, and not so free in giving or receiving love . . .
>Consumed with WHAT MIGHT HAVE BEEN? OR WHAT SHOULD HAVE BEEN?

OR, WAS THERE SOMETHING ELSE . . .A DEATH? ABANDONMENT? SEXUAL ABUSE?
ALL OF THESE THINGS ROB US OF LIVING THE ABUNDANT LIFE IN CHRIST.

We have stuffed things inside of us, buried hurts as life went along; some are emotional firebombs buried alive. And then we wonder why we are not flourishing. I believe it is the reason so many people are sick, physically sick. Medical science has linked stress and sickness, but the unhealthy condition of our emotional/spiritual hearts, including sadness, can also lead to sickness, many times, phantom sicknesses, that doctors just can't seem to diagnose or explain.

We bury our hurt, (stuffing a little more into the rucksacks we drag behind us, getting heavier all the time), sometimes because we just have to get on with life at the time, and somehow do not get back to 'deal with it'. But then something happens, and some one or some thing touches that spot, and like a land mine, it explodes! And we have pieces of ourselves lying all over the place, and it is ugly.

Grab a piece of scratch paper, and interview yourself. 'What have I buried? What have I left unresolved? From what do I need God to set me free? What are the hurts that need healing?' List them.

Your husband or wife walked out on you. How did you feel? Angry, crushed, rejected, lonely. Then feel it, grieve it. Give it to God, ask him to heal it—don't bury it again! God heals the brokenhearted and binds up their wounds. Psalm 147.3. The Lord is good, and his mercy endures forever! Psalm 106.1 His mercy is enough to cover anything that has hurt or wounded you. **It is time to start to heal, get free and really live life!**

From: Christine DiGiacomo, espressocd@cox.net

Subject: In, but not Of . . .Colossians 3.1-3

"Being IN the world, but not OF it" is quite a challenge, but oh so very important if our lives are to be right in Christ. It was Jesus' prayer for us before he went to the cross – that we may be in the world, but not of the world.[1] Paul instructs us to 'think about the things of heaven, not the things of earth . . .' because this life is fleeting, whereas our hereafter is eternal. Always with one eye cast toward Heaven, we then establish our priorities accordingly. "Christians who did the most for the present age were those who thought the most of the next," C.S. Lewis wrote.[2] But, do things we think about, do our daily activities suggest we live for today—'storing up treasures for this world', or rather that we are storing up 'treasures in Heaven where moths and rust cannot destroy—'[3] as Jesus taught us? Hmmm . . . *what things do you do on a daily basis that will last forever?*

The things of Heaven are those which are of Christ, which Paul said to fix our minds upon – those things which are true, honorable, right, pure, lovely, and of good repute . . .on these things, we are to think.[4]

Do you want to please God with your life? Want to have joy? Obey. *Be IN the world, but not OF it.* Paul said, "Since you have been raised to new life with Christ, set your sights on the realities of heaven, where Christ sits in the place of honor at God's right hand. Think about the things of heaven, not the things of earth. For you died to this life, and your real life is hidden with Christ in God." **verses 1-3**

My friends, we are challenged to "walk in a manner worthy of the Lord, to please *Him* in all respects, bearing fruit in every good work and increasing in the knowledge of God."[5] Paul is not suggesting we extract ourselves from everyone or everything that does not profess the name of Christ, rather that we stay in relationship with those who have not yet come to know him, <u>without</u> our values becoming once again those of the world, who do not know Christ . . .so that we are indeed *IN the world, but not OF it.* God has called Christians to play a role by celebrating what's good and true and beautiful, working for change in what isn't, and looking forward in hope to God's redemption of all things.[6]

We're to be morally and spiritually distinct without being culturally segregated.[6] Aye, you and I are to be *IN the world, but not OF it.*

[This is the last thread I wish to extract from Paul's teaching at the start of chapter 3, before we move on; for readers who just joined us, you can read all previous teaching from Colossians at www.pastorwoman.com–most recent Morning Briefings – this is #20 in Colossians series.]

1 – John 17
2 – quoted in Don Eberly, *Restoring the Good Society: A New Vision for Politics and Culture,* **p.80**
3 – Matthew 6.20
4 – Philippians 4.8
5 – Colossians 1.10
6 – Tullian Tchividjian, Unfashionable – Making a Difference in the World by being Different, Multnomah Books, 2012

From: Christine DiGiacomo, <u>espressocd@cox.net</u>

Subject: Things to be killed. Colossians 3.5-10

Being IN the world, but not OF it is quite a challenge, but oh so very important if our lives are to be right in Christ. As Christ followers, our lives should look different than those who do not profess his name. Since that is the case, Paul tells us what to do:

So put to death the sinful, earthly things lurking within you. Have nothing to do with sexual immorality, impurity, lust, and evil desires. Don't be greedy, for a greedy person is an idolater, worshiping the things of this world. Because of these sins, the anger of God is coming. You used to do these things when your life was still part of this world. But now is the time to get rid of anger, rage, malicious behavior, slander, and dirty language. Don't lie to each other, for you have stripped off your old sinful nature and all its wicked deeds. Put on your new nature, and be renewed as you learn to know your Creator and become like him. Vs. 5-10, Ch. 3

Wow! Okay, good instruction. Where to begin?

Again, let me take you to what I know and experience – when a young person (high school) has been consumed with the pressures of the world – drinking, 'sexing', smoking, etc. and then they meet the love of Christ, I see their desire to change. Truly! But how does she then break out of patterns, relationships, and desires that have taken her down the wrong path? The battle always begins in the mind, and ultimately, it is won or lost there as well.

Again . . .Paul, writing to the Romans–Do not conform to the pattern of this world, but be transformed by the renewing of your mind. Then you will be able to test and approve what God's will is—his good, pleasing and perfect will. Romans 12.2 *Be transformed by the renewing of your mind.*

Paul says to renew our minds . . .by RENEW, did Paul mean MAKE NEW? Make our minds new?

By RENEW, did Paul mean REPLENISH, REFILL? Replenish or refill our minds?

By RENEW, did Paul mean ENLARGE, EXPAND? Enlarge or expand the capacity of our minds? The answer is 'yes', all of these things; I think Paul meant for the word to mean all of these, and more!

Commonly, we speak of renewable resources, and our minds would certainly fall into that category.

Spiritual transformation comes about as we change our lives from the inside out. It is the trifecta of the Holy Spirit, the Word and us working together. Our part of RENEWING OUR MINDS comes with action and intention. Jesus said, Seek first the kingdom of God . . .The most important way we can make our minds new, replenish and expand our thinking is by seeking God first. It is the first step in morphing from being CONFORMED to TRANSFORMED.

Then Paul tells us the action we are to take: put to death the sinful, earthly things lurking within you. Have nothing to do with sexual immorality, impurity, lust, and evil desires. Don't be greedy . . .get rid of anger, rage, malicious behavior, slander, and dirty language. Don't lie to each other . . .Paul does not mince words; in fact, he reminds us that sin draws the anger of God.

Do not love the world or anything in the world, the apostle John wrote. If anyone loves the world, the love of the Father is not in him. For everything in the world—the cravings of sinful man, the lust of his eyes and the boasting of what he has and does—comes not from the Father but from the world. The world and its desires pass away, but the man who does the will of God lives forever.*

Dear God, renew our minds with thinking that is set on you—that which is true, virtuous, lovely, and honorable—forgive us for our sins of wanting what the world values, rather than that which is pure and of you. Forgive us for caring more about how <u>we</u> feel and what <u>we</u> want, rather than that which honors you. In the name of Jesus, Amen.

*1 John 2.15-17

From: Christine DiGiacomo, espressocd@cox.net

Subject: Love is . . .Colossians 3.12-14

In the 1970s newspapers, there was a little cartoon strip called **Love is . . .**

It featured a male and female wearing big smiles and nothing else, with a simple line of writing about some aspect of love. I looked for them and cut them out of every newspaper and saved them in envelopes. One of my favorites: **Love is . . .being able to say you're sorry.** Paul's next thoughts could be entitled **Love is . . .so, let's love!**

Take a look: Therefore, as God's chosen people, holy and dearly loved, clothe yourselves with compassion, kindness, humility, gentleness and patience. Bear with each other and forgive one another if any of you has a grievance against someone. Forgive as the Lord forgave you. And over all these virtues put on love, which binds them all together in perfect unity. Colossians 3.12-14

Hmmm . . .how beautiful is that? We are to lead with love, because in Christ, we have been dearly loved. Radically changed by his love, you and I are to *clothe* ourselves with compassion, kindness, humility, gentleness, and patience, and offer forgiveness when needed.

Robbie is 18 years old. Last year, he stepped forward to lead the campus portion of Fellowship of Christian Athletes. Oh, sure, he had met Christ—or so he thought. But mostly, I think if honest, he would say he thought being 'club president' would look really good on his college applications. Many conversations about spiritual growth seemed to sail right over his head. Then a strange thing happened—in the summer between his junior and senior years of high school—he had a personal encounter with Jesus Christ, and it radically transformed him. At our lunchtime club meeting today, when I asked a roomful of sitting-room-only students what was different about Robbie . . .someone yelled from the back, 'Love just comes out of him!'

Would you say your life is characterized by compassion, kindness, humility, gentleness, patience, forgiveness . . .and well, love? If not, then perhaps it is time to spend more time with the Lover of your soul, so that his love will rub off on you. Paul previously described this kind of love for the Corinthians:

Love is patient;
 love is kind.
  Love does not envy;
   is not boastful;
    is not conceited;
     does not act improperly;
      is not selfish; is not provoked;
       does not keep a record of wrongs;
        finds no joy in unrighteousness,
         but rejoices in the truth;
          bears all things, believes all things,
           hopes all things, endures all things. 1 Corinthians 13.4-7
Love is of God.[1]

Love is why God created us in the first place. God did not create us out of need. He created us out of his love.[2] God, who needs nothing, loves into existence wholly superfluous creatures in order that he may love and perfect them.[3]

It is in relationship with God that we learn about love, and the Holy Spirit's presence in us grows us into people who can know and express love. Love is . . .of God, and may it be of us.

1 1 John 4.7
2 John Ortberg, <u>Love Beyond Reason</u>
3 C.S. Lewis, <u>The Four Loves</u>

From: Christine DiGiacomo, <u>espressocd@cox.net</u>

Subject: Let's bring back Grace. Colossians 3.12-14

I always choose my clothes with care; the way I look probably matters way too much. And obviously, I don't leave home without my clothes! Paul tells us that since we are God's children, we should *clothe ourselves* carefully.

"You are the people of God; he loved you and chose you for his own. So then, you must clothe yourselves with compassion, kindness, humility, gentleness, and patience. Be tolerant with one another and forgive one another whenever any of you has a complaint against someone else. You must forgive one another just as the Lord has forgiven you. And to all these qualities add love, which binds all things together in perfect unity." [GNT]

Zoom out with me a moment, and listen as Paul dictates from prison to his scribe, 'Let your gracious gentleness be known to all men.'[1] 'Gracious gentleness' comes from the Greek word, epieikeia. In other texts, the word is used to mean *'graciousness, forbearance, softness, patience, gentleness . . .or a different response than straight-line justice though justice is warranted.'* Paul is admonishing his people to **Be merciful to others.** Friends, the world around us is crying out for mercy!

The common dictionary definition of mercy is 'compassion or forgiveness shown toward someone whom it is within one's power to punish or harm.' More often than not, the term mercy is used interchangeably with compassion, but alas it is <u>more</u> than that! When it would seem like judgment is eminent, the judge decides to pardon instead—he chooses to give mercy. Jesus said, "Blessed are the merciful, for they will be shown mercy."[2] I want to be shown mercy . . .do you?

In order to give mercy, I believe one has to experience mercy. Paul had experienced God's mercy, and so he could teach about it. God wasn't initially so gentle with Paul, knocking him to the ground on the road to Damascus in order to get his attention . . .in order to get him to close his mouth, and open his mind to the truth of Jesus Christ. But it was all to extend to him the tender mercy of eternal salvation. That same salvation message Paul took on the road and across the waters, establishing churches as he went. Paul's message posed a threat to Rome, and landed him in the prison as he writes, 'Rejoice in the Lord, again I say, rejoice. Let your gracious gentleness be known to all men. The Lord is near.'

Christ would say to us, 'Hey Christian, wake up—don't let your pettiness be the reason someone else wants nothing to do with Christianity; don't let your hate-speak drive people from the church. Look for the things you are *for*, not just against. Look for ways to encourage and bless one another in my name!'

Oh, Friends, we are to be light in the world. Light draws and attracts, it does not repel. Be joyful, Christian, and let your joy be seen. Do not be the excuse someone needs to stay away from Jesus, rather be gracious, be merciful, Christian! Look for ways to embrace, to extend compassion, to *include* rather than *exclude*; let your life be characterized by *joy,* and look for ways to give away joy, joy, joy! Let's bring back graciousness in our treatment of one another—like when we accept our change from a salesclerk, when our mate comes home in the afternoon, when our coworker seems uptight and possibly even defensive in manner—let's choose to extend grace.

1) Philippians 4.5
2) Matthew 5.7

From: Christine DiGiacomo, espressocd@cox.net

Subject: Let Peace Rule. Colossians 3.15

Logophile. There, I said it. I am a logophile. Today I am coming out, coming clean, making my confession—I am a logophile. I love words. Learning about them, considering their origins, and endeavoring to expand my own vocabulary–I find it all quite interesting. Do you think differently of me now?

From time to time, looking at several different Bible translations broadens the meaning of the Scripture we are studying. Most times, www.Biblegateway.com enables me to go from one to another, even considering them side by side, or listening to one and then another by clicking on the little speaker symbol at the top.

Take a look with me please at Paul's words to us on peace:

Verse 15–And let the peace of Christ rule in your hearts, to which indeed you were called in the one body. And be thankful.

Look at this please: *"Let the peace of Christ be the decider of all things within your hearts*, for it is to that peace you were called, so that you might be united in one body." The same word Paul used for 'rule' or 'decider' suggests we are to *let the peace of Christ be the umpire in our hearts.* The verb Paul used was derived from the same word used in the athletic arena . . .<stay with me> it is the word that is used of the umpire who settled things in any matter of dispute.[1] *Let the peace of Christ be the decider of all things within your hearts.* Friends, that means if there is a clash of feelings, a stepping on of pride, a pulling in two directions, a rending of our emotions, if we let the peace of Christ be the decider, we will choose the way of love.

In recent days, I wrote, "In order to give mercy, I believe one has to experience mercy." With peace, the same is certainly true. As I prayed this through this morning, I wrote in my prayer notebook, "O God, in order for me to truly be at peace with others, I must gain peace from you [which is my salvation]; in order to be at peace with you, I must learn what it is to abide, and do so; in order to apprehend and live in peace, I must trust you, O God . . .then, and only then can I be an instrument of your peace." In order to let the peace of Christ rule in my heart, I must <u>experience</u> that peace.

Though heads of state endeavor to broker peace in our world, there is only One who brokers true peace.

The only peace that is worthy of the name is **Peace with God**.

God's peace is not man-made,
  can't be learned in a book
    can't be trumped up with enough good will.

Our loving God offers his children a peace which is beyond human understanding! We remember Paul's words to the Philippians: *Do not worry about anything, but in everything by prayer and supplication with thanksgiving let your requests be made known to God. And the peace of God, which surpasses all understanding, will guard your hearts and your minds in Christ Jesus.*[2] His peace makes it possible for you to be in a very difficult situation or relational struggle, and still know peace. Peace that comes from God cannot be adequately or fully described, and it is certainly not available in the world. Yet if I asked you to define God's peace, and you have experienced it, your first thought would etch a smile on your face—your entire countenance would change just thinking about it. Peace . . .sweet peace.

"Our hearts are restless until they rest in Thee." St. Augustine said. And he was right. Jesus is the only source for true peace in our hearts, and we have immediate access to it. **Let the peace of Christ rule in your hearts**.

1 William Barclay, Daily Study Bible–Colossians
2 Philippians 4.6-7

From: Christine DiGiacomo, espressocd@cox.net

Subject: . . .With all wisdom. Colossians 3.16

What is encompassed by wisdom? Socrates was purported to have said 'the only true wisdom is in knowing you know nothing.' I don't buy that actually, unless it is in comparison to the overall scope of what can be known. Regarding wisdom, I find the whole notion of it interesting, her various angles compelling and intriguing. One author penned, 'at one point in my life, I thought the stories of intelligent men who devoted their lives to the pursuit of wisdom and glory transcended the limits of human understanding and showed the best of human abilities. I was wrong. I had the chance to read the lives of several artists and writers and was inspired by their accomplishment. Yet, I was discouraged by their own plot, which they did not have the power to recreate.

Then I asked, what was their wisdom for? If such wisdom would push an artist to kill himself, a writer to become a hermit, or a philosopher to despise his neighbors, then what was their wisdom for? "For with much wisdom comes much sorrow; the more knowledge, the more grief." (Ecclesiastes 1.18) Human wisdom is indeed foolish. The wisdom of the world can never replace the Word of God.'[1]

Hence, Paul wrote:

"Let the message of Christ dwell among you richly as you teach and admonish one another with all wisdom through psalms, hymns, and songs from the Spirit, singing to God with gratitude in your hearts."[2]

This is a beautiful verse! Another look: "Let Christ's teaching live in your hearts, making you rich in the true wisdom. Teach and help one another along the right road with your psalms and hymns and Christian songs, singing God's praises with joyful hearts."[3]

For the Lord gives wisdom, and from his mouth come knowledge and understanding . . .Proverbs 2.6 The world only offers a counterfeit. Real wisdom comes from God. James tells us God will give us wisdom when we ask, and then expounds on the nature of God's wisdom. **But the wisdom that comes from**

heaven is first of all pure, then peace-loving, considerate, submissive, full of mercy and good fruit, impartial, and sincere. Jas. 3.17

True wisdom emanates from the heart of God—it is not prideful or puffed up. But the amazing thing about it is that we do not have to take classes in it or keep searching for the latest cultural iteration of it . . .wisdom can be had by asking God for it. And God will give generously. If we seek to know him, his wisdom, his directions and plans for us, we will be wise—through studying his Word—which takes diligence, I might add—and communing with him.

As the heavens are higher than the earth, so are my ways higher than your ways, and my thoughts than your thoughts. Isaiah 55.8

Remember! The scope of wisdom includes~

>**understanding**–what is true, right, lasting
>**discretion**–the ability to decide responsibly
>**prudence**–wise in handling practical matters, exercising good judgment, common sense, careful about one's conduct
>**discernment**–keen insight
>**knowledg**e–the sum of scholarly learning through the ages; wise teachings of the ancient sages
>**action**–exercising discretion, prudence, discernment in choosing a course of action for ourselves

Because we lack it, let us include in our daily morning time, a prayer for wisdom. Amen.

1–I 'googled' the question 'what is true wisdom?' and this was the source that popped up: www.txtmania.com/articles/**wisdom**.php, from which I quoted several lines
2–Colossians 3.16, NIV
3–Colossians 3.16, Philips Translation

From: Christine DiGiacomo, espressocd@cox.net

Subject: My thoughts, a Melody. Colossians 3.16

Music is powerful . . .indeed, music is so very powerful.
Music seems to have the ability to go to the places inside of us where mere words without melody do not penetrate. Often, when teaching on some topic or another, I use a song to set a tone or a mood . . .sometimes to get folks thinking or musing, or perhaps to unwittingly drop their guard.

Plato wrote, *"Music is the movement of sound*
  to reach the soul
  for the education of its virtue."
I have read it several times, and each time, its meaning grows, as does my understanding!

Since reading Colossians 3.16, I have been enchanted by the latter half of the verse: *Use all wisdom to teach and instruct each other by singing psalms, hymns, and spiritual songs with thankfulness in your hearts to God.*
Music, which incorporated both singing and dancing, goes back as far as one righteous Jewish boy, David, who played his harp and sang to the first king of Israel, Saul. David passionately and unabashedly sang and danced before the Lord. Now I am not a historian of worship or anything, but perhaps David was the first true worshipper . . .lifting his hands, singing, even clapping his hands, as he danced before the Lord! Can you imagine? How scandalous! And so it was from this Judaic tradition that the early Christian church sang psalms and hymns of praise because they had grown up doing so within their strong Hebrew tradition.

Similarly, music played a significant role in the slavery movement in three different arenas: 'spirituals', work songs and recreation songs. Many of these songs of hope gave way to musical styles with which we are familiar: the blues, gospel music and even jazz. How creative is our Creator who gives to his creation good gifts that keep on giving, my dear friends—even when the gift comes out of a time that is hard, a time that is oh, so bad. Surely music is one of his greatest gifts, his greatest talents . . .is it not?

Where do you worship? Is it in the Greek or Russian Orthodox Church? Then, you know the premium that is placed on sacred music! Is it in the liturgy of the Catholic or Episcopalian church? Or how about in the free-form hands-in-the-air setting where expressive contemporary worship music is more likely the norm? Each of these has its own style, each has its own sound. But now I take you back to our text, where Paul wrote:

~Use all wisdom to teach and instruct each other by singing psalms, hymns, and spiritual songs with thankfulness in your hearts to God.

Whatever your style, whatever your Christian tradition, I pray that you will sing to the Lord. It is good, it is right to sing praise to the Lord, who promises that he 'inhabits the praises of his people'.* 'Want to invite God into your gathering? Sing praises to him. 'Want to invite God into the place where you are—your bedroom, your car, your . . .? Sing praises to him. For he inhabits the praises of his people! He does not care if you sing on key . . .he does not care if you can even carry a tune, he hears the tone of your heart. He finds your praises beautiful.

One of the ways I keep myself centered on him throughout my day is listening to music that honors him. If I know the words, I sing along, offering from my heart, pure praise, surrender, and devotion. Music is powerful. It is oh, so powerful because it gives my thoughts a melody.

*Psalm 22.3

From: Christine DiGiacomo, espressocd@cox.net

Subject: Living the Name. Colossians 3.12-17

He said, she said . . .and then they said it back to each other a little louder, and soon they were at it . . .arguing again! 'Not in an intimate relationship? Not to worry! You will have plenty of opportunity to be at odds with someone soon—at work, in the classroom, on your sports team, across the dinner table, in the checkout line at the grocery store, or trying to scratch out a living in a Kenyan or Ugandan village . . .unless you choose otherwise. It is the reason Paul wrote to remind us how to choose the better path, especially since we belong to God. Take a look with me at Paul's charge to us, but be certain to hear his heart in his words—oh, and do savor the words—read as to absorb and let the virtues become a part of your very being:

~ Therefore, as God's chosen people, holy and dearly loved, <u>clothe yourselves with compassion, kindness, humility, gentleness and patience.</u>

~ <u>Bear</u> with each other and <u>forgive</u> one another if any of you has a grievance against someone. Forgive as the Lord forgave you.

~ And over all these virtues <u>put on love</u>, which binds them all together in perfect unity.

~ Let the <u>peace of Christ rule</u> in your hearts, since as members of one body you were called to peace. And be thankful.

~ Let the <u>message of Christ dwell among</u> you richly as you teach and admonish one another with all wisdom through psalms, hymns, and songs from the Spirit, <u>singing to God</u> with gratitude in your hearts.

~ And whatever you do, whether in word or deed, <u>do it all in the name of the Lord Jesus</u>, giving thanks to God the Father through him.

Thank you, Paul, for this is the essence of Christian living.

Are you a person who thrives with a checklist? How are you living and loving in Christ? The checklist Paul provides gives us a great opportunity to take stock of ourselves. Paul said to 'clothe' ourselves with these godly attributes–oh, if only we could just put on a garment that would set us for each day!

Of course, the underlining is mine, designed to help us notice a few things about these verses. True virtuous living finds its origins in the person of Jesus Christ, our teacher, model, Savior and guide. We are meant to live daily with his word alive in our minds. One way we can do so is by singing hymns and songs of praise. (Do you know that the earliest Scripture verses I memorized as a wee child were the ones set to simple melody lines? They are with me to this day: 'Beloved, let us love one another . . .for love is of God and everyone that loveth is born of God, and knoweth God . . .' 1 John 4.7 and 8. Then there was 'Study to show thyself approved unto men, a workman that needeth not to be ashamed, rightly dividing the word of truth.' 2 Timothy 2.15 I could go on, but I won't.)

Finally, in just six verses, Paul mentions the importance of giving thanks three times. It is not just good and right to give thanks to God, but when we choose to be thankful, the way of gratitude breathes new life into our lives. So let's be a thankful people, regularly breathing out our thanks to God throughout the day.

And I guess if we could truly clothe ourselves, we would be doing what Paul told us to do in verse 17: whether in word or deed, we would do it all in the name of the Lord Jesus. So, let's do just that, Friends . . .whatever we do, let us work at it with all our hearts so as unto God, remembering that as Christians, it is his name we bear. Let's bring him glory.

From: Christine DiGiacomo, espressocd@cox.net

Subject: Chosen—A Valentine from God to you.

I hope that the word "chosen" speaks to you. As children of God, we are God's chosen ones. Chosen means you are wanted, your company is sought after.

When I know that I am chosen, I know that I have been seen as a special person. Someone has noticed my uniqueness and has expressed a desire to know me, to come closer to me, to love me. You and I have been seen by God from all eternity . . .as unique, special, precious beings. Hear me as I ask——can you pleeease open up your soul, can you open your mind, open the eyes of your heart that you might be able to take this into yourself—for it is too marvelous for words? **God chose you and me to love him and enjoy his love forever.**

Peter said that followers of Christ are 'a chosen generation' . . .oh, I like that. In our society, though, sometimes the term 'chosen' harkens back to a harder time in life when we remember not ever being chosen—like in recess playground games. Hmmm . . .Janis Ian's song runs through my mind—you know, about learning the truth of not being chosen—"to those of us who know the pain of valentines that never came, and those of us whose names were never called when choosing sides for basketball . . ."

To be chosen as the Beloved of God is something radically different. As God's <u>chosen</u> people, holy and dearly loved, clothe yourselves with compassion, kindness, humility, gentleness and patience. Instead of excluding others, it includes others. Instead of rejecting others as less valuable, it accepts others in their own uniqueness. It is not a competitive, but a compassionate choice.

To associate 'being chosen' with competitiveness would be looking from the world's point of view, right? Instead, let us look at our Heavenly Father's point of view: he chose you, he chose me. Before the foundations of time, (as we think of time, not him, because he sees time all at once), it was his heart that we would be his. God did not send his Son for a race of people, only men, or for 144,000 witnesses . . .no, Jesus came for all, because ALL ARE CHOSEN. But don't think less of being chosen because <u>he came for all</u> . . .he chose you individually. Remember, he knit you together in your mother's womb, he knows the number of hairs on your head, he knows the length of days of your earthly existence, and your name is written on the palm of his hand—that's how specifically he thinks of you.

Yet, there are those who have been left behind, abandoned, and rejected in life, and accordingly, cannot quite comprehend what it would really feel like to be chosen. Did your mother give you up for adoption, and it hurts you in a very deep, private place inside yourself to this day? (even though you are fifty years old!) Did your boyfriend decide he didn't want to be with you anymore when he found out he might have responsibility for his unborn child you were carrying? Did your father abandon the family when the pressures became too great, and so you've never really trusted a man again? Did your wife choose to 'be' with another man over you? 'Oh God,' our hearts cry out, 'how do I heal? How can I ever really trust?' Yet, he knows. Remember, Judas, Peter, and Thomas had all walked, learned, and been with Jesus for more than three years, and yet they rejected him. 'You think God doesn't know the hurt in your heart because his own men un-chose him?

In the midst of these and other extremely painful realities, we have to dare to reclaim the truth that we are God's chosen ones, even when our world doesn't choose us. We cannot let others determine whether or not we are chosen . . .Our preciousness, uniqueness, and individuality are not given to us by those who meet us in clock-time—our brief chronological existence—but by the One who has chosen us with an everlasting love, a love that existed from all eternity and will last through all eternity. "I have loved you with an everlasting love; therefore I have drawn you with lovingkindness." Jeremiah 31.3

You are a chosen one . . .loved, cherished, and adored; further, God takes great delight in you. Chosen—that is just too marvelous for words!

~reference: Life of the Beloved, Henri Nouwen

From: Christine DiGiacomo, espressocd@cox.net

Subject: Right thinking about self is critical–Colossians 3.12

As God's chosen people, holy and dearly loved, clothe yourselves with compassion, kindness, humility, gentleness and patience.

Right thinking about self is critical to getting along with others. If humility might be defined as 'a right position of our hearts toward God, toward others, and ourselves' . . .how do we get aligned properly?

Illustrations are always helpful when we are seeking to see clearly. Once I was teaching on this topic, and asked my friend, Liz, to bring in a piece of her art to make my point. Liz is talented in many forms of media, but this particular sculpture is my favorite one of her creations. 'Tis a beautiful sculpted figure of a woman, finished in a soft blue, with strands of precious stones, cascading in shades of translucent aqua's to form an elegant skirt. I just love it! After unveiling it, I took comments and opinions from the audience about the piece . . . but then, I invited Liz to step up and tell us what she had in mind when she created the lovely lady. The Artist's thoughts were different from those of the observer. Not surprisingly, the thoughts of the Creator are quite different from ours.

>If we want to have a right orientation of our hearts to God, others, and self, then we ought to let our Creator inform our thinking.

"About that time the disciples came to Jesus and asked, 'Which of us is greatest in the Kingdom of Heaven?' Jesus called a small child over to him and put the child among them. Then he said, 'I assure you, unless you turn from your sins and become as little children, you will never get into the Kingdom of Heaven. Therefore, anyone who becomes as humble as this little child is the greatest in the Kingdom of Heaven." Matthew 18.1-4

So Jesus wants us to be as humble as a child? Yes. A little child is not proud or arrogant because the world has yet to corrupt him. A child has no problem expressing himself, saying what he wants or needs. He trusts simply and easily. That is how our Heavenly Father wants us to be with him.

Somehow, I think we might see our greatest struggle with humility in our attitudes toward other people. The 'proud' are often: critical, boastful, angry, vengeful, arrogant, prejudicial, greedy, self righteous, and judgmental; whereas, the 'humble' give the benefit of the doubt, practice quiet confidence, forgive easily, believe in the Golden Rule and being courteous, patient, teachable, and free from pretense.

Paul wrote that we should "Be completely humble and gentle; be patient, bearing with one another in love." Ephesians 4.2 As God's chosen people, holy and dearly loved, clothe yourselves with compassion, kindness, humility, gentleness and patience. Colossians 3.12 "Do nothing out of selfish ambition or vain conceit, but in humility consider others better than yourselves. Each of you should look not only to your own interests, but also to the interests of others." Philippians 2.3-4 What can be added to that? *Each of you should look not only to your own interests, but also to the interests of others.* So, let's give the benefit of the doubt, let's assume we really don't know everything, and let go of our critical spirits, okay?

As for how we view ourselves – well, it is God who created us and gifted us. He alone can give us our true value! We are not capable of a proper estimation, and we certainly should not let anyone else give us our value . . .only God. We are loved by God our Creator.

He takes great delight in us, and will quiet us with his love.[1] He made us in his image.[2] We are the apple of his eye.[3] And when we fell from grace, he gave us the very best he had—his own precious Son—to restore us to him.[4] So we should view ourselves as loved by God. I am who I am because he loves me, not because of anything I have done. (Not much room for pride there.) On the contrary, when I begin to understand God's grace to me, it makes my heart swell with gratitude; and I've noticed that gratitude and humility are often companions.

Learning to live in the reality of who we are in Christ settles the question of our worth, and frees us up to be humble . . .it frees us up to be like children.

1 Zephaniah 3.17
2 Genesis 1.26
3 Zechariah 2.8
4 John 3.16

From: Christine DiGiacomo, espressocd@cox.net

Subject: Clothe yourselves with h u m i l i t y. Colossians 3.12

How would you quantify the difference between worldly wisdom and the wisdom of God?[1] Consider this statement: A person who is wise also must be humble because a wise person recognizes his creaturely dependence upon God. Hmmm. "Who is wise and understanding among you? Let him show it by deeds done in the humility that comes from wisdom."[2] Interesting . . .in that verse, James anchors humility in wisdom. And then a few verses further he says, "But he [God] gives us more grace. That is why Scripture says, "God opposes the proud but gives grace to the humble."[3] We have been looking at Paul's instructions to Christians to be clothed in, among other things, humility. There is no doubt—God highly esteems humility. "Lord, teach us about humility, won't you?"

Humility . . .The elder President Bush praised Ronald Reagan's humility in his eulogy. In 1981, Reagan was recovering from the gunshot wound he received during the assassination attempt. It seems that just days after the surgery that repaired his life-threatening injuries, his aides discovered him on his hands and knees in his hospital room, wiping water from the floor. Bush said of Reagan, "He worried that his nurse would get in trouble". *humility.*

Humility–another one of the words that captures a spiritual concept and value that the world does not value or teach much about. Humility is sometimes difficult to grasp, and often misunderstood. It is not being self-effacing; it is not a lack of confidence; it is seeing ourselves in correct position before our Maker and with other people. What do you think of your position before the Lord? Where do you place your own value in regard to others? Who are the 'others'? Others are those I know and love, those I just know, those I know and don't esteem too highly, those I don't know at all. How do I treat these others? It has been said that 'the sign of a gentleman is how he treats those who can be of absolutely no use to him.'

The Scriptures hold out humility as a virtue to be sought after, a quality to embody, a discipline to be practiced and honed. It is revered in both the Old and New Testaments. About 800 years before Christ was born, at a time when Israel and Judah had risen to heights of economic affluence, yet had fallen to depths of spiritual decadence, the prophet Micah penned, "What does the Lord require of you? To act justly and to love mercy and to walk humbly with your God."[4]

Then there was Moses, about whom God said, "more humble than anyone else on the face of this earth."[5] Think of it—God used this humble man to lead the Israelites out of Egypt, parting the Red Sea for them to escape the pursuing Egyptian armies. God used Moses to continue to lead the people, entrusting to him the 10 Commandments. Moses—humble>>> then God honors and exalts him. That is a pattern repeated in Scripture. What did Jesus have to say about humility? Hmmm . . .it is good. In Matthew 18, to answer the disciples' question, "Which of us is greatest in the Kingdom of Heaven?" Jesus called a small child over to him and put the child among them. Then he said, "I assure you, unless you turn from your sins and become as little children, you will never get into the Kingdom of Heaven. Therefore, anyone who becomes as humble as this little child is greatest in the Kingdom of Heaven." The disciples were left standing there, scratching their heads, having to consider what it was about that child . . .

So, what is it about a child? A friend who told me once that what really turned on his quest for Christian truth was his young daughter's faith. Why? Children trust more simply, love with abandon, are not spoiled by the 'wisdom' and teaching of the world; children are teachable.

Let's pursue humility today, my friends; let's teach our children to be humble and embody it in the workplace . . .indeed, let's clothe ourselves with humility.

1 – Justin Borger of the Generous Giving staff
2–James 3.16
3 – James 4.6
4 – Micah 6.8
5–Numbers 12.3

From: Christine DiGiacomo, espressocd@cox.net

Subject: Why All this Talk about Humility?
Colossians 3.12

Clothe yourselves with h u m i l i t y, Paul said. Why am I hammering the point home about the importance of humility? Because when we are humble, we have better relationships; simply put, if we possess some portion of humility, we are more likely to get along well with others. Have you looked ahead in Colossians chapter 3? Paul is about to get specific about all of our relationships, beginning with the most intimate of them . . .marriage! In order to consider 'getting along', humility—right thinking about one's self in relation to God and others—is fundamental.

Humility and the fear of the Lord bring wealth and honor and life.[1] True humility comes from a place of strength and inner security. Genuinely humble people who have a desire to seek the well being of others are generally very secure people—fully aware of their gifts, training, experience, and all of the attributes that make them successful. Honest, healthy self-assessment results in more than healthy self-assessment; it results in more than a humble constitution; it translates into actions that can be observed, actions that others will want to emulate.[2]

'Ever notice someone who is truly humble? Study him . . .why is he like that? Perhaps it is partially his attitude. Consider this: Your attitude should be the same as that of Christ Jesus: Who, being in very nature God, did not consider equality with God something to be grasped, but made himself nothing, taking the very nature of a servant, being made in human likeness. And being found in human appearance as a man, he humbled himself and became obedient to death—even death on a cross![3] Isn't it interesting that Paul said 'have the same attitude' as Jesus—wait a second, is humility an attitude? (look up 'attitude' in your dictionary—did Paul say this right? Is humility an attitude?) Then it should be easily changed, correct? I think it is a matter of seeing the value of HUMILITY, putting a premium on it personally, and again, <u>seeing our rightful place before God</u>.

Remarkably, no matter what was said or done to Jesus, he was unbelievably humble. Again, what an upside-down economy from ours! Whoever is the least among us will be the greatest[4] . . .huh?

We cannot underestimate the impact of cultural values pressing in about us at all times—trying to shape us . . .trying to mold us. Whereas, Paul warned us, 'do not be conformed to this world, but be transformed . . .'[5], or as the Philips translation states, 'do not let the world squeeze you into its mold'!

We remember that Jesus told the arrogant Pharisees, who had a puffed-up, improper view of self, that the greatest commandment was 'to love the Lord with all our heart, soul, mind, strength . . .and love our neighbor as ourselves.'[6] Paul elaborates on this when he says, "Do nothing out of selfish ambition or vain conceit, but in humility consider others better than yourselves. Each of you should look not only to your own interests, but also to the interests of others."[7]

Again, the common dictionary definition says pride is: a sense of one's own proper dignity or value; self-respect. Where do we get proper dignity? It is the realization we are nothing, and we have nothing, but by the grace of our Creator. Did you choose your height? Did you choose your family of origin or place of birth, realizing most of us were born in freedom? 'O, no you di'nt, child!'

You are a person of worth because you are loved by God, extended his grace, and invited into relationship with him forever! That is what gives you your worth; we have no basis for arrogant pride. Instead, let us put others' needs and feelings above our own—let's move toward humility.

Humility . . .so much to think about, but first we must value it, highly esteem it, and desire to be about it ourselves so that we will be teachable, quietly confident, patient, teachable, good listeners, courteous, forgiving, and known for giving others the benefit of the doubt.

Ah, humility . . .first, we need to recognize its value, and then we need to purpose to bring it back.

1 Proverbs 22.4
2 Chuck Swindoll, So, You Want to be Like Christ?
3 Philippians 2.5-8
4 Luke 9.48
5 Romans 12.2
6 Mark 12.30-31
7 Philippians 2.3-4

From: Christine DiGiacomo, espressocd@cox.net

Subject: It is not about you.

All this talk about humility, and clothing ourselves in it. As I type, I have an uppercase C, K, H, G, and P penned in dark green ink on the inside of my wrist, just above my watchband—hoping it will aid my memorization, as well as remind me that because I am chosen, and therefore holy and dearly loved, I am to clothe myself in compassion, kindness, humility, gentleness and patience. Apparently, this discussion—particularly on humility—has reso- nated with many, as I have heard from you! Honestly, in my most recent study and examination of the whole matter of humility – I have begun to think <u>humility is perhaps the most fundamental piece of living rightly</u> as we are meant to live and love. When we do as Paul suggested, and in humility, consider others better than ourselves . . .not operating out of selfishness or conceit . . .it means we think of others first. It means we are more concerned with their feelings and well being than our own. > Friends, this impacts every area of our lives, from getting along in families and cooperating well with work associates to driving a motor vehicle in traffic, to playing on the athletic field!

There is a beautiful story of a young man with a disability who was running in the Special Olympics. He got to the hundred-meter race and was running like crazy for the gold medal, when he saw one of the runners near him had slipped and fallen. Without hesitating, he turned around and picked him up, and they ran across the finish line together . . .last. Humility?

It is up to each of us to discover how he or she is called to be more fully 'clothed in Christ', in order to serve our brothers and sisters with love, kindness, and humility . . .Jesus insists that his disciples wash one another's feet, remember? It is an act of humility that truly expresses in a very concrete way our love and respect for others.*

"After that, he poured water into a basin and began to wash the disciples' feet, and to wipe them with the towel with which he was girded."

His actions symbolized spiritual cleansing, but also after having washed their dirt-caked, sandled feet, he went on to teach them:

"So when he had washed their feet, taken his garments, and sat down again, he said to them, "Do you know what I have done

to you? You call me teacher and Lord, and you say well, for so I am. If I then, your Lord and Teacher, have washed your feet, you also ought to wash one another's feet. For I have given you an example, that you should do as I have done to you. Most assuredly, I say to you, a servant is not greater than his master, nor is he who is sent greater than he who sent him. If you know these things, blessed are you if you do them." From John 13

How much time do you spend serving? And, do you do it with a cheerful heart? You can, you know. As our beloved Paul suggested, you might do so by singing 'psalms, hymns and spiritual songs, with gratitude in your hearts to God. And whatever you do, whether in word or deed, (even laundry), *do it all in the name of the Lord Jesus, giving thanks to God the Father through him.'* Here's a little thought about serving with a cheerful heart—"Laundry, laundry, laundry . . .there is never an end!" I sometimes think. Now, when I fold my family's clothing, I realize it is not just for them I toil; <u>a serving heart honors God</u>. And, while I am doing laundry . . .it is a wonderful time to pray for each person, as I match socks, fold underwear, etc. 'See the opportunity? 'See the difference in the attitude of serving?

We cannot love well without humility, because to love another means it can't always be about us!

*influenced by Jean Vanier, <u>Essential Writings</u>

183

From: Christine DiGiacomo, espressocd@cox.net

Subject: Of household affairs . . .Colossians 3.18-25

Submit. *Love. Obey. Do not aggravate. Serve. Work. These are the commanding verbs of today's focus–as Paul turns to the relationships of the household.*

"Wives, submit to your husbands, as is fitting for those who belong to the Lord. Husbands love your wives and never treat them harshly. Children, always obey your parents, for this pleases the Lord. Fathers, do not aggravate your children, or they will become discouraged.

Slaves, obey your earthly masters in everything you do. Try to please them all the time, not just when they are watching you. Serve them sincerely because of your reverent fear of the Lord.

Work willingly at whatever you do, as though you were working for the Lord rather than for people. Remember that the Lord will give you an inheritance as your reward, and that the Master you are serving is Christ. But if you do what is wrong, you will be paid back for the wrong you have done. For God has no favorites."
Colossians 3.18-25

Your attention, please? Historical understanding of cultural context is critical to the correct interpretation of this Scripture passage. Women have wanted to exhume Paul's body and kill him again for his command to women: submit to your husbands. [Perhaps they had not had good teaching on humility?]

But understand this—the men of Paul's day must have been even more outraged with his teaching! Women in the first century were just the possessions of their husbands. They had no legal rights whatsoever, and that was true of the Jews, Greeks and Romans. It was Jesus who taught a different way, and Christianity, which sought to implement respect for women into the culture, and love for wives into the marital relationship. Jesus was a revolutionary with regard to his treatment of women! You must be aware that in the first century, at every synagogue service, Jewish men prayed, "Blessed art thou, O Lord, who has not made me a woman." Women sat in a separate section, were not counted in quorums, and were rarely taught the Torah. In social life, few women would talk to men outside of their families, and a woman was to have no close contact with any man but her spouse.[1]

Paul said 'submit' to the wife, but to what and to whom was she to submit? A loving husband. Did you see it? Paul commanded husbands to love their wives . . .a ridiculous notion for a first-century man who thought he could treat his wife however he wanted, even divorcing her for any cause. The Greeks believed that husbands could have as many relationships outside of marriage as they wished, while the wife was to remain chaste. The privileges belonged to the husband and all the duties to the wife in the first century.[2]

Christianity ushered in a change—a beautiful change to the whole idea of marriage—love and respect were now in the house. Love? Paul had previously defined love as that which is patient, kind, never jealous or envious, self-seeking, arrogant or rude[.3] "Husbands, love your wives, just as Christ loved the church and gave himself up for her," he taught.[4] Paul is telling husbands to love their wives so much that they would be willing to DIE for them. Now, of who is more required? Wives are to submit because they love, but husbands are to die because they love.

Children were under the total domination of their parents in the ancient world. Roman law permitted a father to do anything he wanted with his children—sell them into slavery, use them as laborers on his farm, or even sentence them to death. Again . . .all privileges and rights were on one side, all duties on the other. So Paul's teaching is absolutely radical.

Now do you see the reason for such focus on humility? If there is humility present in a loving marriage, there is a mutual obligation of serving one another. If humility is in the house, love can abound, respect flourish. Get radical in your humility . . . audacious in your love . . .crazy in your submissiveness.

1 Philip Yancey, <u>The Jesus I Never Knew</u>
2 William Barclay
3 1 Corinthians 13.4-7
4 Ephesians 5.25

From: Christine

Subject: Devoted. Colossians 4.2

Devote yourselves to prayer with an alert mind and a thankful heart. Colossians 4.2

devote – give yourself to

To what do you devote yourself in life? Might be to:

-raising your child/children in a loving home
-being a good person
-making enough money to retire at a certain age
-bringing attention to a particular cause (i.e. breast cancer)
-maintaining a healthy, vital marriage
-staying young looking and feeling . . .
all of which, if we are devoted, require maximum effort on our parts in order to bring about-

Whereas, God's call for us to be devoted in prayer is about our pressing into him in such a way, that he will act on our behalves. David wrote, 'Delight yourself in the Lord, and he will give you the desires of your hearts.'[1] What a concept—God Almighty will bring about the desires of our hearts, as we pray in faith to him.

The words that Paul uses here in Colossians 4.2 for 'devote yourselves' is *proskartereite,* and is suggestive of a gritty determination not to give up until God's response comes. 'Devoted to raising proper children? Carry them to the Lord in prayer, and be relentless in praying for them. Do you have a child who is far from God, floundering in a sea of poor life choices? Devote yourself to praying for her. Lock arms with Jesus, and he will intercede before the Father on your child's behalf[2], and be tireless in your prayer. Is your marriage strained, ready to break apart? How much time have you devoted to praying for your mate, to asking God to come and do what only he can do?

When we work, we work; but when we pray, God works, it has been said. But there is even more cause to be devoted in prayer. *"As you grow in prayer, God will reveal more of himself to you, breathing more of his life into your spirit. Mark my words—it will be the most filling and rewarding part of your experience with prayer, more so even than the answers to prayer you are sure to receive. Fellowship with God, trust, confidence, peace, relief – these wonderful feelings will be yours as you learn how to pray."* (from a book that has really inspired me to pray, *Too Busy not to Pray*[3])

Prayer changes us; it grows us to be more like Christ, which also breathes new life into all aspects of our lives, especially those to which we are devoted.

Notice with me the devotion to prayer in the first days of Christianity: "These all with one mind were continually devoting themselves to prayer, along with *the* women, and Mary the mother of Jesus, and with His brothers."[4] It was right after Jesus had ascended into Heaven, and they did what they knew to do, what he had told them to do—they prayed. And as they prayed, the Holy Spirit bound them together. The disciples and Jesus lovers kept at it; they did not tire as they sought God side by side. The writer of Acts tells us in the next chapter, "They were continually devoting themselves to the apostles' teaching and to fellowship, to the breaking of bread and to prayer . . ."[5] Can I tell you something? I love this verse. I wish I could time travel back and fall into one of their evenings together. Picture the men and women as they studied, prayed, ate together . . .sweet, powerful, desirous of all they could get from God, passionate, committed to being together as they discovered what life in the Holy Spirit was meant to be. Yeah, I want some of that.

Devote yourselves to prayer. Prayer connects you with a holy, powerful, loving God who delights in communing with you, and answering your prayers.

1 – Psalm 37.4
2 – Romans 8.34
3 – Too Busy not to Pray, Bill Hybels
4 – Acts 1.14
5 – Acts 2.42

From: Christine DiGiacomo, espressocd@cox.net

Subject: Come. Colossians 4.2

I read what you wrote about being devoted in prayer, and I liked it; I felt sort of beckoned by it. You had the verse at the top– *Devote yourselves to prayer with an alert mind and a thankful heart.* Colossians 4.2 I am challenged by those few words actually. Then when you described that prayer gets God working on our behalf, and us working sort of on his behalf – well, that makes prayer personal. But personally, I just find it hard to be faithful to pray. I know I should . . .I feel better when I do . . .but somehow I am pulled in so many directions, that I rarely just sit down to be with God. Usually, when I pray, I am in a hurry, and sorry to say, but most of the time—well, I just shoot one-liners up, and I hope God is listening. If I am honest with myself, my prayers bore me, and they probably bore God. Can you help?

I sought the Lord. 'Lord, you talked a lot about praying, and I know you want us to pray, but . . .your people need help. And Lord, what did you mean by *Devote yourselves to prayer with an alert mind and a thankful heart?*'

Come to me.
Come often.
Come desirous to be with me, and for me to be with you.
Come open
    ready to receive.
Purpose to bring your best self
    not fuzzy or distracted, but focused on the business of prayer.
No matter the hour or the time of day
I am here to meet with you, and I always bring all of me to be with you.
Do you not know, have you not heard, that I never tire, never slumber or sleep? When you sleep, I continue praying on your behalf to the Father.
When you are unsure of what to pray, my Spirit devotedly prays for you.
But Child, even when you are unsure of what to pray,
    Come.
    Come be with me.

Sit in my presence.
Thank me for loving you, for taking great delight in you.
Thank me for never leaving you.
   Yes, Lord. . .I shall Lord, so be it.
"I thank you God for making me in your image.
I thank you God for knowing me, for knowing all about me,
   and loving me anyway.
I thank you God for making a way for me to be with you forever,
   By giving me Jesus.
I thank you God that you are good, and your mercy and kindness are forever~
~you are trustworthy
~you don't change
~your love does not fail, it does not fade
~you don't change your mind or go back on your word
~you have a plan and a purpose for me

And then Lord, I thank you that when I fail, when I sin, I can turn around and come to you, admit my sin, you will forgive and cleanse me . . .you no longer see that sin in me.
   And Lord, I thank you that I will one day hear you say, 'Welcome home, Child . . .wait till you see all I have here for you, wonders you have never even imagined will be yours, and the love just flows on and on. You were made for this, your home has been prepared. Welcome, my beloved.'

Just call me 'devoted' as I will come.
Amen.

Come boldly to the throne of our gracious God. There we will receive his mercy, and we will find grace to help us when we need it most. Hebrews 4.16

From: Christine DiGiacomo, espressocd@cox.net

Subject: Prayer makes a difference. Colossians 4.2

Devote yourselves to prayer with an alert mind and a thankful heart.

Friendship with anyone requires a couple things—desire to know the person, and some way to make that happen. Friendship with God is no different. We must get to know him—who he is, and what he is like—and the best we can get to know God is by reading what he wrote to us—what he thinks of us, his plan for our lives and for eternity—all of which we can find in the pages of **Scripture**. And . . .friendship with God requires communication. We call communication with God '**prayer**'.

And for you and me, prayer ought become as vital to our existence as is breathing. Let me give us the benefit of the doubt, and say that, at best, 'we under-utilize prayer—we under-access it'.

Some people seem to constantly be seeing answers to prayer—have you noticed that? Do you want to see answers to your prayers? Well, while there are no formulas, there are a few things to consider:

1) Pray to God in <u>Jesus' name</u>—there is power in that name, and it is a privilege to be able to call on it!
2) When you pray, <u>BELIEVE</u> that you will receive. James 1.6-8
3) Consider your <u>conscience</u> and your heart—are they pure before God?

Otherwise, your prayers may be ineffective. Are you harboring unforgiveness or bitterness in your heart? The psalmist says it simply, "If I regard sin in my heart, the Lord will not hear."[1] "Dear friends, if our hearts do not condemn us, we have confidence before God and receive from him anything we ask, because we obey his commands and do what pleases him."[2]

4) Finally, we are to pray according to <u>God's will</u>. (We can know what is consistent with his will through studying his Word) When God's will is unclear, then we let the Holy Spirit pray on our behalf. 'The Spirit intercedes for God's people in accordance with the will of God.'[3] Yeah, prayer makes a difference.

Pray . . .For everyone who asks, receives. Everyone who seeks, finds. And to everyone who knocks, the door will be opened.[4] Indeed, 'Seek the Lord and his strength; Seek his face evermore!'[5]

As has been said, 'prayer changes things', and besides that, it changes you and it changes me. ' . . .You do not have because you do not ask.'[6] Let's ask, let's pray! It is well worth pushing past our 'go, go, go' mentality, 'must keep going, must keep going' . . .'prayer, me? Of course I do—I pray at meals, when I need something, for my kids . . .is that what you mean?' Well, yes, but do you spend time just communicating with God—in a give and take kind of conversation? That's what I think builds friendship with him—yeah, time with him—just you and him. Mano e mano – one on one. Prayer makes a difference.

1–Psalm 66.18
2 – 1 John 3.20-21
3 – Romans 8.27
4 – Matthew 7.8
5 – 1 Chronicles 16.11
6 – James 4.2

From: Christine DiGiacomo, espressocd@cox.net

Subject: What is Prayer, really? Colossians 4.2 – Devote yourselves to prayer . . .

What is your definition of prayer? Talking to God? Sure. But the first time Scripture recorded someone talking to God, it was Eve, lying to him, in Genesis 3.10. Was that prayer, then? Not really. So perhaps we need to broaden our description of prayer . . .let's give it some thought.

This prayer of David in Psalm 5 really speaks to me~ *Give ear to my words, O Lord, consider my meditation. Give heed to the voice of my cry, my King and my God. For to you I will pray. My voice you shall hear in the morning, O Lord; in the morning I will direct it to you, and will look up.*

I notice several things from David's prayer ~ he went to God **in the morning** at the start of his day. Morning prayer is vital to who I am throughout the day. Notice with me that David rightly ordered his position, and **surrendered himself** by saying, 'O Lord,' 'my King and my God'. David knew that God was his strength. In order to come into prayer fully expectant of meeting God, we must endeavor to think rightly about God. As A.W. Tozer said, *"What comes into our minds when we think about God is the most important thing about us."* I believe we must realize something about **God's character**, and about **His abiding love for us** . . .Oh, we won't be able to fully grasp either, but we must try!

God is wild about you; he thinks you are delightful; he considers you to be fearfully and wonderfully made. *You* might notice that your biceps aren't as big as they were in college, while your waist size is bigger—but *he* doesn't really notice. God is interested in you, at your core . . .

It is one of the greatest mysteries in this life to contemplate just what his love for us might mean, if only we could grasp it. Unfortunately, we have let others be the 'keeper of the keys' as to our worth. We have let others interpret God's character to us, instead of investigating it on our own, searching out Scripture, and pouring ourselves into developing an ever-deeper experiential relationship with him. God's storehouses are limitless, his attention able to meet with each of us individually, and his desire to talk with us in prayer ever incredible.

Tomorrow, why not start your day with some special time alone with your Father in prayer? There is nothing like being connected with God.

From: Christine DiGiacomo, espressocd@cox.net

Subject: Quiet Space enables you to Hear.
Colossians 4.2

It usually takes some 'quiet' to hear . . .

I have found that **creating order** in my prayer time is a way of making my prayers more complete. From the prayer our Lord gave us, we can make an acronym; while there are several, I should like to offer you mine. A.C.A.T., from a message I delivered to a high school group about 16 years ago entitled, "How to skin A CAT"—a message on prayer.

A is for Adoration–take a moment to start your prayer by giving God his 'due'; praise him for who he is.

C is for Confession–search yourself, and ask God to show you anything you need to confess and turn away from.

A is for Asking–for your needs, and for the needs of others.

T is for thanking God for his good gifts to you—for your health, God's Word, Heaven, your spouse, your children, your job, sunshine, hope, grace, forgiveness, mercy, new days . . .you get the idea.

When I am able, I like to write my prayers in a small, lined notebook, using **A.C.A.T.** to stay focused. Then I am present with my pen, and my mind is not apt to wander. The notebook also serves as a record of God's unending faithfulness in my life. Figure what works for you . . .it is worth it.

A few years ago, I added another letter to my model – "L" for Listening. Do you think God still speaks? Have you heard his voice? If you did, would you know it was God?

I love what the boy Samuel said to God, when he thought he heard his voice–"Speak, Lord, for your servant is listening." (1 Samuel 3.8-9) If God was indeed speaking, he wanted to hear him . . .me, too! I didn't grow up understanding that God speaks to his children today, but instead that I would only find his voice in the pages of Scripture. And yet, inside myself, it only made sense that God had not stopped communicating his thoughts once the

Bible was complete. To be sure, the 'permanent address at which the word of God may be found is the Bible,' but since the canon of Scripture was closed almost 2000 years ago, does that mean he has nothing to say to us in the 21st century? I think not.

Do you desire to hear God's voice? I would think you do if you are desirous of a meaningful relationship with him. In the scriptures, we find God spoke to those who were seeking after him—Moses, Noah, Mary, Esther, Isaiah, Saul (Paul), Ezekiel and others. 'The ideal for hearing from God is finally determined by who God is, what kind of beings we are and what a personal relationship between ourselves and God should be like.'[1]

How does God speak?

~in a still, small voice
~through Scripture
~through other believers—including messages from the pulpit
~visions—when awake
~dreams—when asleep
~circumstances—opened or closed doors; serendipitous meetings
~a "knowing" in our innermost being

When God speaks, he expresses his mind, his character, and his purposes—and his leading will always be consistent with Scripture. He will not shout at us though, in order to get a word in . . ."we need to give much time to communicate with the Holy Spirit. He will not speak to anyone who is in a hurry.[2] God is a gentleman and will not break the door down to get our attention, so we do well to obey—

"Be still, and know that I am God."[3]

Ah, therein lies the 'catch' for most of us . . .it takes discipline to be still, and to quiet our minds. Create some 'quiet' in your prayer time for the Lord to speak. Make a decision to 'be still' throughout your day—turn the radio off in your car . . .go for a walk outside with no i-pod or headphones.

Create some quiet in your day, and 'be still, and know that he is God.'

1) Dallas Willard, Hearing God–** a phenomenal book;
2) David Wilkerson
3) Psalm 46.10

From: Christine DiGiacomo, espressocd@cox.net

Subject: Shhh . . .God has something to say to you.

> Colossians 4.2–*Devote yourselves to prayer with an alert mind* . . .
> Pray . . .be alert so you can hear God's voice.

And behold, the Lord passed by,
  and a great and strong wind rent the mountains,
    and brake in pieces the rocks before the Lord;
      but the Lord was not in the wind~
      and after the wind, an earthquake;
but the Lord was not in the earthquake~
  and after the earthquake, a fire;
    but the Lord was not in the fire~
      and after the fire, a still small voice.
                    1 Kings 19.11,12–KJV

We have been looking at the sweetness of our personal prayer lives—communicating our hearts and lives with God—and then learning to listen for his voice as well. I love how the Lord came to Elijah in the above passage—*in the still, small voice* or *a gentle whisper,* as another translation says. Folks are keenly interested in discerning the voice of God, though most have not been taught too much on the subject . . .so let's step a little closer. Is there anything we can do to ready ourselves to hear from God? I believe there is.

>Be desirous of God—want more of God in your life. Or, as Jesus said, "**Seek first his kingdom**."[1]
  It should not be that our primary goal is to hear the voice of God; on the contrary, it should be our purpose to engage in a **loving relationship with God**. **'Interesting to note that *before* God spoke in the still, small voice to Elijah in the passage above, Elijah said, "I am zealous for the Lord God Almighty." Hmmm . . .am I zealous for God? Are you?

>Get rid of anything that stands between you and God, and might obstruct God's message. **Confess your sins to him,** confident that he then forgives you.

>Be a person in the Word. The primary address at which the word of God may be found is the Bible. More of God's speaking to me has come in conjunction with study and teaching of the Bible than with anything else. **The Bible expresses the mind of God** since God himself speaks to us through its pages. [2]

>Be attentive; listen–be aware, be desirous

>Make quiet your friend

>Appropriate 'listening' into your prayer time–**A**doration; **C**onfession; **Listening; A**sking; **T**hanking

So, you feel that God has spoken to you in some fashion, **how do you know it is God's voice**, and not your own, or another's? Check:

—Is it consistent with sound biblical teaching?
—Is the *voice gently leading,* or is it commanding and harsh?

God's voice gently guides and encourages, giving hope–Psalm18.35 God leads; Satan drives—John 10.4
God convicts; Satan condemns and brings guilt—Psalm 8.12. God woos; Satan tugs hard
When God speaks, he does not use fear to motivate. If fear overcomes you, it is the enemy, not God—2 Timothy 1.7[3]

—When you are trying to ascertain what God is saying to you, look at circumstances, the Bible, and inner impulses of the Spirit.

Do you think most people want to hear God's voice? People want to hear from God when they are in desperate need of help, needing to be rescued or given direction for a big decision—but what about as a matter of course? Do you?
God wants to be wanted . . .to be wanted enough that we are ready and predisposed to find him present with us.
I don't want to miss his gentle overtures.
Shhh . . .listen. God has something to say to you.

1 Matthew 6.33
2 Dallas Willard and me!
3 Elizabeth Alves, The Mighty Warrior

From: Christine DiGiacomo, espressocd@cox.net

Subject: When God seems A.W.O.L. . . . Colossians 4.2

A number of years ago, I remember feeling like God was A.W.O.L. in my life. Truly, I felt like my prayers were hitting a rubber ceiling and bouncing back. I wondered if I had done anything to make God mad at me . . .but in short order remembered that God is neither moody nor temperamental.

God has promised he will never leave you, but your ability to feel him or hear from him might be dimmed. So, if you want to maintain an awareness of God's presence in your life,

refrain from activities that would "grieve" him.

To grieve God is to hurt the heart of God. It hurts when you reject him, and turn toward that which you know is out of line with his will for you . . .like <u>sin</u>.

What is sin? I often get that question. 'Sin' includes those things that God has clearly laid out as such—envy, murder, stealing, hatred, idolatry, etc., and also that which we feel in our conscience is wrong, and we do anyway. (For more on that, consult Romans 7 as Paul describes the struggle within.)

Another thing that hurts the heart of God is our <u>disobedience</u>. Jesus said, "If anyone loves me, he will keep my word . . ."[1] And the writer of Ecclesiastes said, "Fear God and keep his commandments, for this is the whole duty of man."[2] I love these thoughts:

"Obedience is not the major work of the disciple; it is the only work."[3]

"There are only two things required of the disciple (student) of Jesus Christ: to love God and to obey him."[4]

What else grieves the heart of God? <u>Lack of repentance</u> – when you have erred—overtly or in your heart, and have left it unresolved or unconfessed. Oh, the grace of God covers all . . .through it, we have guilt absolved, and debts removed.

<u>Hardness of heart or judgment</u> toward others is not pleasing to God, and may cause us to feel a separation from him. Let's put off a spirit of fault-finding and criticism, and "If possible, as far as it depends on us, live at peace with everyone"![5]

Another thing that makes the presence of God less apparent to us is <u>preoccupation with self</u>. If there is too much of me, there will be too little of him. Let's 'have this attitude in ourselves which was also in Christ Jesus—who didn't require equality with God something to be grasped, but emptied himself. . .'⁶ What attitude did Jesus have? HUMILITY. Have this attitude in yourself: humility. (Ah, sweet humility)

"Okay, I'm good on all of these areas, but I still don't FEEL the presence of God—does that mean he is not there?" No, it does not mean that. Here is the thing about the Christian faith—at some point in our lives, we must decide that God and his Word are trustworthy, and if he says that 'he is with us' then we can stand on the promise as truth—and that truth has little to do with how we **_feel_**. "Never will I leave you, never will I forsake you . . ."⁷

God's presence in my life is a constant, and I am daily trying to 'abide in him' just as he told the disciples to do in John, chapter 15. I love to picture Jesus gesturing to a familiar grape-vine as he said to them, "Abide in me, and I will abide in you." Abiding involves training and disciplining ourselves—guarding our hearts and minds, and what we put into them—to remain close to the Lord.

One day, when we see Jesus face-to-face, we shall no longer have to discipline ourselves to 'abide' or 'remain' in him, for we will be with him, never to be separated again. O, what a glorious day! Until then, let's remember that, no matter how we FEEL, God will never leave us or forsake us. God has not gone A.W.O.L.

1 John 14.23
2 Ecclesiastes 12.13
3 Calvin Miller
4 George MacDonald
5 Romans 12.18 Amplified
6 Philippians 2
7 Hebrews 13.5

From: Christine DiGiacomo, espressocd@cox.net

Subject: Zooming Back Out. . .Colossians 4

We have been studying Colossians 4.2, "Devote yourselves to prayer with an alert mind and a thankful heart . . ." looking closely at how we can get to know our God more intimately and stay daily connected to him through prayer . . .but it is valuable to look at this verse in the context of Paul's letter, set here in its last chapter. The J.B. Phillips translation is insightful, as it words things quite powerfully~

"Remember, then, you employers, that your responsibility is to be fair and just toward those whom you employ, never forgetting that you yourselves have a heavenly employer.

2) Always maintain the habit of prayer: be both alert and thankful as you pray. Include us in your prayers, please, that God may open for us a door for the entrance of the Gospel. Pray that we may talk freely of the mystery of Christ (for which I am at present in chains), and that I may make that mystery plain to men, which I know is my duty.

Be wise in your behavior toward non-Christians, and make the best possible use of your time. Speak pleasantly to them, but never sentimentally, and learn to give a proper answer to every questioner.

Tychicus (a well-loved brother, a faithful minister and a fellow-servant of the Lord) will tell you all about my present circumstances. This is partly why I am sending him to you. The other reasons are that you may find out how we are all getting on, and that he may put new heart into you. With him is Onesimus one of your own congregation (well-loved and faithful, too). Between them they will tell you of conditions and activities here.

Aristarchus, who is also in prison here, sends greetings, and so does Barnabas' cousin, Mark. I believe I told you before about him; if he does come to you, make him welcome. Jesus Justus, another Hebrew Christian, is here too. Only these few are working with me for the kingdom, but what a help they have been!

Epaphras, another member of your Church, and a real servant of Christ, sends his greeting. He works hard for you even here, for he prays constantly and earnestly for you, that you may become mature Christians, and may fulfill God's will for you. From my own observation I can tell you that he has a real passion for your welfare, and for that of the churches of Laodicea and Hierapolis.

Luke, our beloved doctor and Demas send their best wishes.

My own greetings to the Christians in Laodicea, and to Nymphas and the congregation who meet in her house.

When you have had this letter read in your church, see that the Laodiceans have it read in their church too; and see that you read the letter I have written to them.

A brief message to Archippus: God ordained you to your work—see that you don't fail him!

My personal greeting to you written by myself. Don't forget I'm in prison. Grace be with you.

PAUL"

Here's my charge to you: whatever God has you doing, do it well! Do not fail him—work at it with all your heart.

From: Christine DiGiacomo, espressocd@cox.net

Subject: Use your words well. Colossians 4.2-4

How do you use your words?

I challenge you today to become a person who uses more words to be thankful, to pray, to encourage others, to bless . . .

Looking to God's Word: "Devote yourselves to prayer with an alert mind and a thankful heart. Pray for us, too, that God will give us many opportunities to speak about his mysterious plan concerning Christ. That is why I am here in chains. Pray that I will proclaim this message as clearly as I should." Colossians 4.2-4

These are Paul's closing admonitions to the Christians at Colosse – Give yourselves wholeheartedly to prayer! And in your prayers, carry me to God-as a minister of the gospel-that though I am in prison now, I will continue to have opportunities to tell the life-changing message of Jesus Christ. And please—pray that I will proclaim this message clearly!

Oh Friends, I pray that you too will devote yourselves to prayer! I pray that you will see with the eyes of your heart the value of communing with the God of the universe, who created all that ever was and shall be, and yet loves you individually. And in your seeing, that you will pray in the morning as the psalmist did, offering your day to God for his wisdom, direction and care, and then that you will keep an open line of communication all the day long.

Pray for the teachers, pastors, missionaries who have given themselves to the spreading of the good news of Jesus Christ. Lift them before the Father, praying they will be faithful and clear, handling the Word of God. (Humbly, I ask for your prayers; my goodness, if Paul wanted prayer, how much more do I need prayer in the sharing of the Gospel and the teaching of God's Word!)

Notice with me that Paul did not ask that he would be released from prison . . .huh, that is quite incredible. Rather, he asks that he would make the most of his opportunities to share Christ. Think of it, each Roman guard to whom Paul was chained would hear the life-saving, transformational message of Jesus Christ, 'live and in person' from the world's greatest evangelist himself. Paul did not waste any chance he had to share Jesus.

And yet again in his letter to the Colossians, Paul stresses the value of being thankful. Thankfulness is a choice on our part. Should we choose it, thankfulness can be not just an attitude shift, but a state of being, a mode of operation, a lens through which we see the world. Scripture holds gratitude as a value to be grasped and lived out. Certainly, staying mindful of our many blessings for which we carry 'thanks' in our hearts is key to knowing contentment in this life.

"Now thank we all our God, maker of Heaven and earth . . .while much is uncertain on a daily basis, we know who holds the future, and we know who holds our hand.

We look to You, O God, and lift our hearts in thankfulness to our great God.

Daily, we underestimate your power; often, we fail to note how you are working around us. . .

We thank you, Lord, that you would choose to involve us in your work; we thank you that indeed you cause all to work together for good to those who love you.

Thank you for life and breath and strength—we offer ourselves to you this day." Amen and Amen

From: Christine DiGiacomo, espressocd@cox.net

Subject: The Power of your Words. Colossians 4.5-6

My dad was a redheaded Oaky who came to California in the Dust Bowl. Soon after arriving in a small farming town, his father deserted the family, leaving behind a poverty-stricken saint of a woman, and seven young children. Cleatis Leon Todd (my dad's name . . .can you imagine?) grew up tough in Tulare County, often eating fruit from nearby orchards to leave any potatoes or beans for the rest of the family. Was it the abandonment of his father that made my father's heart so hard? I will never know . . .but this I know, his critical words hurt me deeply. And then one day when I was about 14 years old, my dear mother shook her finger at me and said, 'if you're not careful, you're going to be just like your dad—always critical.' Mom's words were both a curse and a blessing; they shocked me, got my attention, and caused me to purpose changing what might have been my 'natural bent'. What trait of the tongue did you inherit—loose talk, coarse talk, a critical tongue? Or do you have lips quick to gossip, and a steady flow of negative spew?

Take a look at Paul's thoughts:

"Live wisely among those who are not believers, and make the most of every opportunity." *And then, look at this:* "Let your conversation be gracious and attractive so that you will have the right response for everyone." Colossians 4.5-6

Consider **the power of your words**! For with your mouth, you will speak life, you will tear down or simply offer drivel. 'Let your conversation be gracious and attractive so that you will have the right response for everyone.'

Apt. Suitable. Beneficial. Gracious. Encouraging. Do those adjectives describe the things you have to say? Scripture has much valuable instruction to influence our taming of the tongue, such as: *A gentle answer turns away wrath, but a harsh word stirs up anger.*[1] *By your words you will be justified, and by your words you will be condemned.*[2] From the wise teacher, Solomon- *There is a time for everything, and a season for every activity under heaven: a time to be silent and a time to speak*[3] (notice the order: time to be silent, time to speak-- hmmm) . . .and *Do not be quick with your mouth, do not be hasty in your heart to utter anything before God. God is in heaven and you are on earth, so let your words be few. Let my words be few.*[4]

Let my words be few. Huh . . .that is a really good line, and quite challenging. Too often, I give my opinion when it isn't solicited; too often, I say the unnecessary thing; too often, I use my wit to get attention. Too often, I speak when I have nothing <u>beneficial</u> to say. Consider this, also from Paul, *Let no unwholesome words ever pass your lips, but let all your words be good for benefiting others according to the need of the moment, so that they may be a means of blessing to the hearers.*[5] It raises the bar, does it not?

When I was a little girl and my mother had heard too much from me, she would turn and say, "Shhh—keep still now." Indeed, if you have nothing beneficial to say, that is a good word, 'shhh—keep still now.' On the other hand, if you have a word of encouragement, speak it out; if you have a word that affirms, share it! If you have a word that will lighten another's load, offer it—because *pleasant words are a honeycomb, sweet to the soul and healing to the bones.*[6]

1 *Colossians 15.1*
2 *Matthew 12.37*
3 *Ecclesiastes 3.1, 7*
4 *Ecclesiastes 5.2*
5 *Ephesians 4.29*
6 *Proverbs 16.24*

From: Christine DiGiacomo, espressocd@cox.net

Subject: Doing Life Together. Colossians 4.7-18

" . . .That you may stand firm in all the will of God, mature and fully assured." v.12 "The righteous should choose his friends carefully." Proverbs 12.26

Who notices when you aren't there? Who encourages you to keep the faith when you are discouraged? When you are sick, does anyone call to check on you? If you moved out of the area, would you leave a void, or would no one likely notice? Has anyone 'been there' for you when life tossed you about, when you did not know up from down? Hmmm . . .

On the other hand . . .may I ask, WHO do **you** encourage? Have YOU recently reached out to lend a hand, or send a note, to someone who is hurting? When is the last time YOU brought a meal to someone in need? Do **you** SPEND much time praying for the heartfelt needs of others? Have **you** had the opportunity to extend the handshake of 'welcome' to another lately? Have you walked alongside' friends who have weathered the rough storms of life, and seen them through to the other side? I mean, how often do YOU GIVE of yourself to others? Hmmm . . .

Friends, one could see the last verses of Colossians as 'throw-aways', verses that have no meaning or application for us today, since they include a lot of strange names and commendations . . .Not so. Paul's final thoughts written to the Colossians were about his friends and companions—the people with whom he 'did life'.

With a little research we find out something about the people Paul mentions, and their relevance to us today—

Tychicus was to supply a firsthand report of Paul's welfare and his heart toward the young Christians Paul has been teaching. Paul commends Tychicus as a faithful minister alongside him, calling him a 'beloved friend'. Paul thought so highly of him that he would later send him to Crete and to Ephesus to represent him.

Along with Tychicus is Onesimus, both of whom were chosen to carry this letter to the Colossians as well as the letter to the Ephesians.

Onesimus had been a runaway slave who had come from Colosse, and Paul is sending him back to them, commending him as both faithful and beloved. 'Forgive him, welcome him back, as he met your same Jesus when we met here in Rome!'

'Aristarchus sends his greetings.' Aristarchus had been with Paul for the long haul—whether it meant the Ephesian riot, or the shipwreck on the way to Rome (Acts 27), or imprisonment. He lived out his commitment to Jesus Christ through his faithfulness to Paul and the sharing of the Gospel. He was a friend that 'sticks closer than a brother'.

'Luke the beloved physician sends you his greetings.' Ah Luke . . .author of the gospel that bears his name and the book of Acts—(more than a quarter of the New Testament writing!) 'O, the places he could have gone!' Why, his brilliant detail-oriented mind could have taken him anywhere in the Greek or Roman world, but he stayed with Paul—to the very end.

Several others are mentioned—namely Epaphras, who devoted himself to praying for young believers without ceasing. Epaphras was faithful to carry those to whom Paul had ministered the gospel, those for whom Paul was so burdened, to the Lord, interceding on their behalf. Paul counted on the prayers of Epaphras.

Remarkable! These were the men who 'did life' with Paul—loyal friends and laborers in the work of Paul; they were invaluable in his life, enabling him to do what he did for Jesus Christ. They were his **community**. Friends, are you part of such a community? If you are, then thank God, and remain active in it—do your part. From the start of the Christian church, it was how Christians were meant to live together—loving one another, praying and worshipping together, and taking care of one another. In such a community, there is accountability and support, encouragement and sharpening . . .there is LIFE!

From: Christine DiGiacomo, espressocd@cox.net

Subject: Looking back at Colossians.

Well, here we are, having just finished studying Colossians. We have taken two months to look at Paul's letter to the church at Colosse, moved by the love of Paul for young Christians he had never even met.

Remember? Paul conveys his heart as he writes from a Roman prison, 'live a life worthy of the Lord and please him in every way: bearing fruit in every good work, growing in the knowledge of God' (1.13). Paul teaches the utter supremacy of Jesus Christ as the 'visible expression of the invisible God. He existed before creation began, for it was through him that everything was made, whether spiritual or material, seen or unseen.' (1.15-16)

And admonishes us to stay the course—'stand firmly in the truth of the gospel and do not drift,' (1.23) warning not to let anyone take us 'captive through hollow and deceptive philosophy, which depends on human tradition and the elemental spiritual forces of this world rather than on Christ.' (2.8) Instead, Paul said, 'Since you have been raised with Christ, set your hearts on things above, where Christ is, seated at the right hand of God. Set your minds on things above, not on earthly things.' (3.1-2)

You, my friends in Jesus Christ, are *chosen*. . .chosen by God. 'Therefore, as God's chosen people, holy and dearly loved, clothe yourselves with compassion, kindness, humility, gentleness and patience. Bear with each other and forgive one another if any of you has a grievance against someone. Forgive as the Lord forgave you. And over all these virtues put on love . . .' (3.12-14) Surely, these verses should be a mandate for Christian living! By the way, did you don your 'kindness underwear' when you got dressed today? Memorize that verse, Friends—as a note to self: 'clothe myself with compassion, kindness, humility, gentleness and patience.' Yes, yes, yes!

'**Submit**. Love. Obey. Do not aggravate. Serve. Work.' and 'Whatever you do, work at it with all your heart, as working for the Lord, not for human masters.' (3.18-25) 'Devote yourself—give yourself to—prayer with an alert mind and a thankful heart.' (4.2) Because when we work, we work, but when we pray, God works! Prayer is an expression of who we are . . .a living incompleteness . . .a gap, an emptiness that calls for fulfillment.[*]

Prayer moves the hand of God, and lets us know he did not leave us alone in this world, to 'go it' without him. "Come," the Father bids us . . ."Come and meet with me, because I am here to meet with you." Give God some quiet in your life, and listen for his voice—it may come through his still, small voice, it may come in a dream, a 'knowing' deep within you, through other believers, and always—God's heart is conveyed to you from the pages of Scripture.

'Live wisely among those who are not believers, and make the most of every opportunity' to tell others of the great love of God for them.' (4.5) Do you make the most of opportunities to tell others about Jesus—about how different life can be, when lived with Jesus, for him, and in him? Oh, how empty the life that does not have God in it . . .how vacuous, how meaningless.

'Let your conversation be gracious and attractive so that you will have the right response for everyone.' (4.6) How powerful are your words! Why, every time you speak, you might speak life—words of encouragement, or indictment—words of criticism or spite, something with meaning, or that which is meaningless. Choose well.

And finally, Paul signs off his letter to the Colossians, sending greetings and commendations for those whom he valued, because even when imprisoned, community mattered to Paul. Friends were the instruments of God to minister and care for him. I pray that you have good friends, and I pray that you are a good friend! As surely as God gave Jonathan to David, he has a friend or friends in mind for you, my dear ones.

Good Bye, Colossian brothers. How blessed you were to be loved and taught by Paul!

* – Thomas Merton

CPSIA information can be obtained at www.ICGtesting.com
Printed in the USA
BVOW11s0414250913

368230BV00003B/6/P